Ultimate Autos

By Tom Stewart

Published by
Kandour Limited
Monticello House
45 Russell Square
London WC1B 4JP
UNITED KINGDOM

This edition published in 2007 by
CHARTWELL BOOKS, INC.
A division of BOOK SALES INC.
114 Northfield Avenue
Edison, New Jersey 08837
USA

First published 2006

10 9 8 7 6 5 4 3

Author: Tom Stewart
Editor: Mark Holmes
Design and Layout: Susan Holmes
Ultimate Autos Concept: Kaspa Hazlewood
Production Management: Karen Lomax

ISBN-13: 978-0-7858-2127-4
ISBN-10: 0-7858-2127-9

Printed and Bound In China

Foreword

Cars are tools. They have a simple job, to move people and stuff from place to place. But some cars, the cars in this book for instance, are so much more than that. Of course, they can still move people and stuff from place to place, but they're also works of art, sculpture that would not look out of place in any gallery. They are also triumphs of engineering, examples of how man can always go one step better. But best of all, they hit the 'fight or flight' g-spot. When you bury the throttle and their huge engines gird their loins for an assault on the road ahead, you are not simply a man in a car. So far as the ancient core in your brain is concerned, you are back at a time before fire, being chased by a wild animal.

You're on an adrenalin rush.

That said, the man who wrote this book, Tom Stewart, does not allow himself to be sucked into pyschobabble. Tom is the least ambiguous man in the world. I'd say a car has a 5-litre engine. Tom would tell you that, in fact, it's 4,792cc [292 cubic inches]. I would say Tom has ginger hair. Or orange. He'd describe it as burnt umber. So, while this book may be about the sleekest and the daftest and the most expensive cars, Tom has approached them in the same way that you would expect a brain surgeon to approach your daughter's head. With great care and lots of attention to detail.

Jeremy Clarkson, March 2006

Contents

Prices/Currencies: All prices and exchange rates were correct at the time of writing. Prices for cars sold in both the US and UK are quoted at their local retail price. Cars sold in either the US or the UK have their local prices converted accordingly. Some cars from continental Europe have their price quoted in euros, this being the purchase price and required currency at the factory, excluding local/additional taxes/duties. Prices for older cars mentioned have been converted at the average exchange rate for their year of manufacture. While every effort has been made to ensure accuracy, both prices and exchange rates are subject to constant change and the Editors, Publisher and distributors cannot be held responsible.

Weights: Kilos have been converted to pounds and vice versa, using this formula: 1kg = 2.2lb or 1lb = 0.45kg. (The US and Imperial pound is now one and the same.)

Gallons: There is just one reference to gallons (Maybach Exelero, miles per gallon) but the Author admits to not knowing whether this is a US or Imperial measure. (1 imperial gallon = 1.2 US gallons.) Either way, 2.4mpg is pretty thirsty.

Introduction

The history of ultimate automobiles goes back as far as the history of the car itself. The first ultimates were the world's first motorized carriage, designed by Gottlieb Daimler and Wilhelm Maybach, and Karl Benz's patented 'motor car'. Both surfaced in 1886 and, like no invention before, the car was to change life irrevocably, suddenly thrusting personal mobility into another dimension.

The first Cadillac was built in 1902. Named after Antoine de la Mothe Cadillac, the French explorer who had 'discovered' Detroit in the early 1700s, the single-cylinder car was taken to the New York Automobile Show where 2,286 orders were received before the firm declared mid-week that the Cadillac was 'sold out'.

Rolls-Royce was founded in 1906, and soon after this inception its 7-liter, 6-cylinder Silver Ghost was confidently advertised as 'The Best Car in the World'. With co-founder and chief engineer Henry Rolls proclaiming: "Strive for perfection in everything you do. Take the best that exists and make it better, and when it does not exist, design it," few dared to argue.

Having studied sculpture and built cars as a teenager, Ettore Bugatti started building a small, lightweight racer in 1909. When it appeared at Le Mans in 1911 it looked like a toy among giants, but Bugatti finished second and the legend was born. Bugattis went on to win more races than any other maker, scoring over 1,000 victories in 1925 and 1926 alone. In the early 1930s Bugatti built six enormous Royales – arguably the ultimate auto of all time.

In January 1919 Walter Own Bentley established Bentley Motors and by October the first 3-liter was built. Within two years the car was winning races, within six it had set the world 24hr record at an average of 95.03mph, and by 1930 Bentley cars had won the Le Mans 24 Hour race five times. Although Bentley built its reputation on the track, its core business was in luxury sedans.

> " *Strive for perfection in everything you do.* "
> *Take the best that exists and make it better,*
> *and when it does not exist, design it*
>
> **Henry Rolls**

The Maybach 12 made its debut in 1929 and was powered by the world's first volume-manufactured 12-cylinder auto engine. Originally this V12 displaced 6,922cc (422 cu in), but the super-luxury Zeppelin model of 1931 was powered by an even bigger 7,922cc (483 cu in) version producing 200bhp—an incredible figure for the time.

Having founded the Scuderia Ferrari Alfa Romeo race team in 1929, Enzo Ferrari built the first car bearing his name in 1947. It was a 12-cylinder 1,500cc (92 cu in) racer and it won the Rome Grand Prix on only its second outing. Since then Ferrari has produced a constant flow of glamorous supercars, and scored over 5,000 race victories and 14 Formula One Constructors' World Championships.

Professor Ferdinand Porsche's first car, the 356, appeared in June 1948. His father had designed the Beetle under duress, so young 'Ferry' had much to live up to. Often hailed as the world's greatest sports car, the 911 was introduced in 1963 and, several generations later, remains in production today. Since 1970 Porsches have clocked up a record-breaking 16 victories in the Le Mans 24 Hour race.

After Ferruccio Lamborghini crashed his modified 750cc Fiat into a roadside café during the 1947 Mille Miglia road race in Italy, he quit racing and made his fortune making farm machinery. Lamborghini enjoyed his Ferraris, but when Enzo Ferrari dismissed a complaint he'd made about one, the tractor baron hatched a plan; he founded Automobili Ferruccio Lamborghini SpA in 1963 and the brand has been a thorn in Ferrari's side ever since.

What follows are accounts of 32 of the ultimate automobiles of today. I don't claim it to be a definitive list, but it's a pretty fine selection, and serves as my humble tribute to the truly talented designers, engineers and craftsmen who created them.

Tom Stewart - March 2006

Gran Turismo

G.T.: A sporting, enclosed car which combines the features of both sedan and sports car, with excellent styling, performance and handling. Offers good comfort whether in two-seater or 2+2 configuration.

Aston Martin Vanquish S

Bentley Continental GT

Bristol Fighter

Brabus McLaren SLR

Aston Martin
Vanquish S

Power and beauty are a thrilling combination, especially in the form of such a powerfully beautiful car as this. It is guaranteed to turn heads, but that second look had better be quick because the Vanquish S has 200mph-plus potential...

This is the car that launched Aston Martin into the new millennium. When it first showed the Vanquish in 2001, the English company had a proud and long-earned reputation for building luxury GT cars packing serious punch.

Those cars, such as the Vantage of the late '70s and the Virage of the '90s, were brawny but low-tech brutes. Aston Martin needed a new flagship model to move the company into the modern era of advanced electronics and composite materials.

The Vanquish achieved this mission, emerging as a triumph of technology and styling. It even managed to match the film-star achievement of its ancestor, the DB5 of the mid-'60s, by getting James Bond back into the driving seat of an Aston Martin in the 2002 movie Die Another Day.

Aston's new top-line car tapped into techniques developed by race engineers for the Formula One world championships, a series which features some of the most technologically advanced racing cars on the planet. The Vanquish's main body structure uses a combination of carbon-fiber, extruded aluminum and composite materials, all bonded together to form a central monocoque passenger cell, with the exterior panels constructed from 'super-plastic' or pressed aluminum.

The six-speed, close-ratio manual transmission is linked to an electronic drive-by-wire throttle and operated by shift paddles fitted to the steering column, as in a Formula One racing car. The car's

electronic control system monitors and records the mechanical performance of the entire vehicle and can process two million commands per second.

All this technical wizardry was designed to help the driver get the most from the Vanquish's glorious six-liter (362 cubic inch) V12 engine. If, however, the driver is more in the mood for relaxing than racing, the transmission can be set in 'auto' mode, leaving the electronics to deal with the gearshifting.

The Vanquish wasn't just a beautifully-presented showcase for technology, though — it was also one seriously fast car, with 190mph top speed potential. So some serious running gear was included in the package to help keep everything in check.

Ventilated and drilled Brembo anti-lock brakes provided the necessary stopping power, with the steering dealt with by variable-ratio power assistance. The car's independent suspension systems featured forged aluminum wishbones with cast aluminum suspension uprights up front.

The rear axle came equipped with a mechanical, limited-slip differential and an electronic traction control system. Even the Yokohama tires fitted to the Vanquish were designed exclusively for the car, and came complete with electronic tyre pressure and temperature monitoring.

With its classy combination of seductive curves (left) and an intimidating grille (right) the Vanquish leaves a simultaneously attractive and intimidating impression

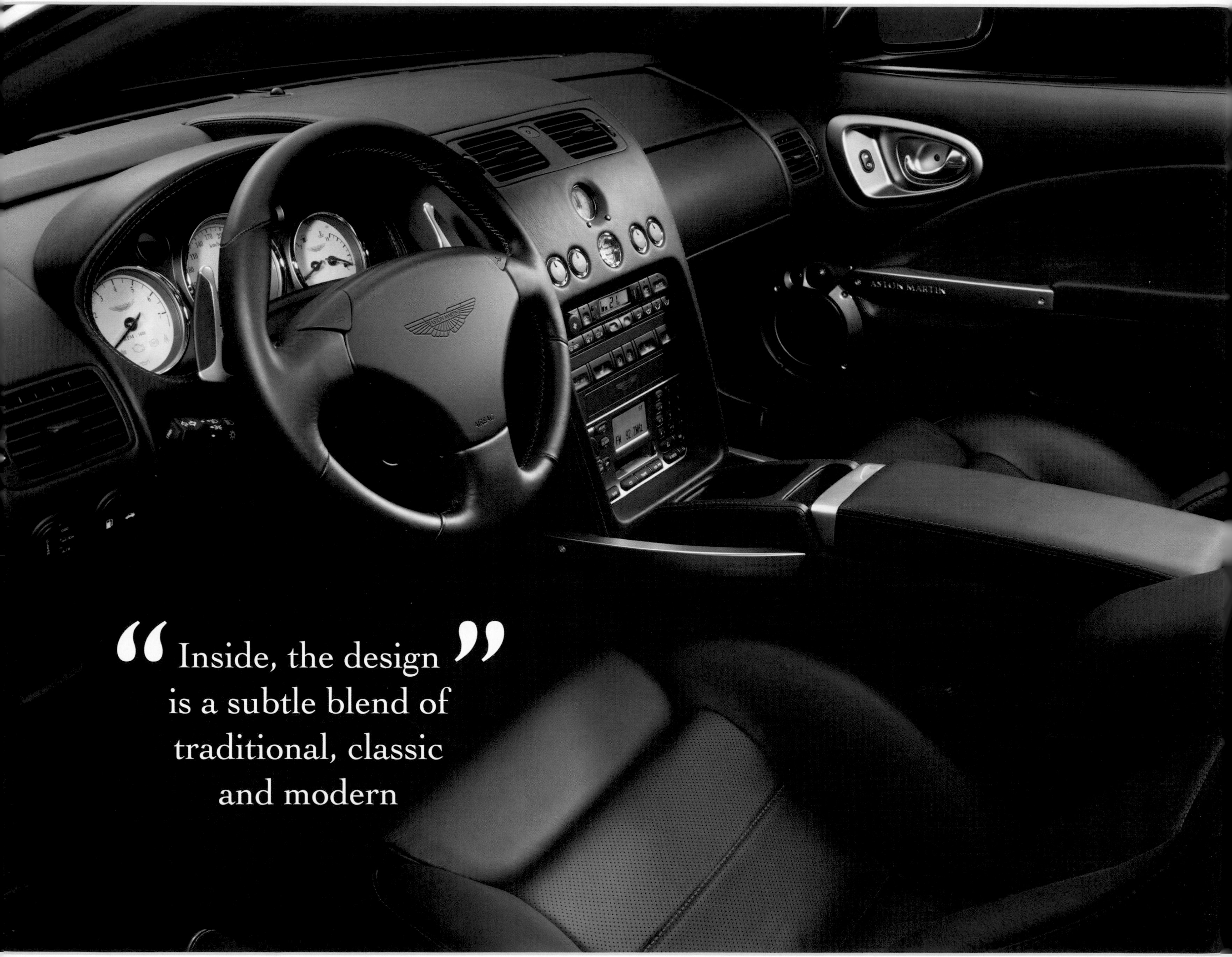

“Inside, the design is a subtle blend of traditional, classic and modern”

Traditional English Connolly hide is matched to modern metal fittings while an old-fashioned starter button shares the dashboard with a multi-lingual onboard trip computer

The result of all this is a car with swift steering response, huge grip in corners, strong brakes and taut but supple suspension which does a specially good job of dealing with imperfect roads. Needless to say, straight-line speed is exhilarating, while the soundtrack of that big V12 engine is guaranteed to grab attention.

The sound is totally unique—more akin to the urgent howl of a racing superbike than a big-vee car engine—and Aston Martin were so proud of it, they recorded it onto disc. Early Vanquish press kits came with a four-minute audio CD filled with angry, high-revving Vanquish noises.

Inside, the design is a subtle blend of traditional, classic and modern. English Connolly hide upholstery is matched to contemporary metal interior fittings and finishes. Following on from Bentley's lead, a prominent red starter button was a nod to days of old, but it can share dashboard space with an optional satellite navigation and an on-board trip computer that can relay information to the driver in 11 different languages. The Vanquish had truly brought Aston Martin into the 21st century.

But time stands still for no man, or car, so at the 2004 Paris Motor Show Aston Martin first showed the Vanquish S, a 520 horsepower version, to be sold alongside the stock Vanquish. With a maximum speed in excess of 200mph, the Vanquish S delivers even greater performance, along with a few subtle suspension and steering changes and some interior and exterior styling revisions.

Further development of the all-aluminum V12, which boasts four overhead camshafts and 48 valves, upped power from 460 to 520bhp, with torque also up from 400 to 425lb/ft. The engine modifications include new cylinder heads with fully machined inlet ports and combustion chambers to improve airflow, revised engine mapping and new fuel injectors. The end result is that the Vanquish S can demolish the zero to 60mph sprint in 4.8 seconds, which shaves two tenths of a second off the stock car's time.

The steering response and brakes have also been upgraded, and with Sports Dynamic suspension they complete the package that pushes the 'S' one step further than the original Vanquish.

Those are the mechanical facts of the matter, but, like all great cars, the Vanquish S is much more than the sum of its parts. ✖

SPECIFICATION	
ENGINE TYPE	V12
DISPLACEMENT	5,935cc (362 cu in)
POWER	520bhp @ 6,500rpm
TORQUE	425lb/ft @ 5,000rpm
TRANSMISSION	Six-speed manual with auto shift
0-60mph	4.8 seconds
TOP SPEED	200mph
PRICE	$255,000 (£174,000)
www.astonmartin.com	

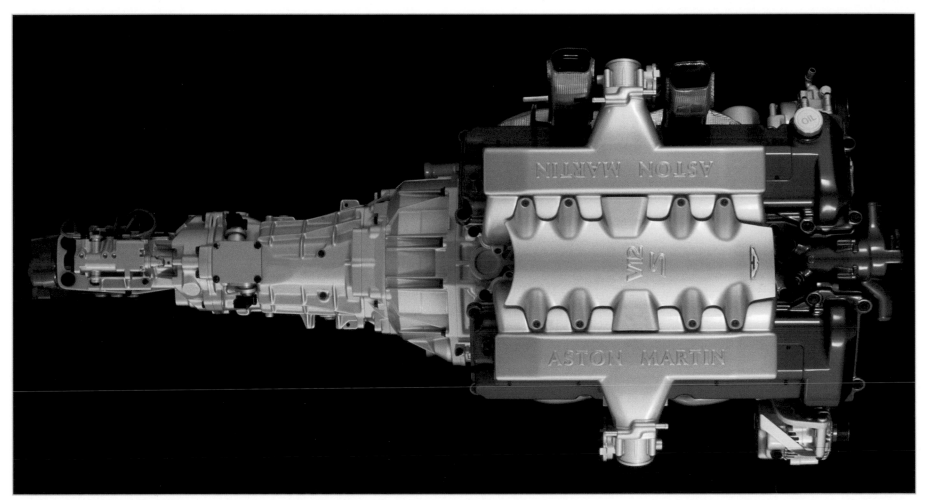

The Vanquish's all-aluminum engine has 12 cylinders, four overhead camshafts and 48 valves. It produces 460bhp in stock form, with the tuned 'S' version giving 520bhp

Bentley
Continental GT

" A potent and unique **"**
driving experience

Bentley has conveyed the essence of English gentlemanly motoring for decades. The Continental GT is no exception, even though a German company paid for its development

*I*magine a Cadillac built by Nissan. It may sound like an impossible notion, but so did the idea of a Bentley manufactured by Volkswagen until the Continental GT was revealed to the world at the Paris Motor Show of 2002.

Its powerful visual impact was pure Bentley, but under the skin it was German technology which provided the driving force and German finance which provided the backing for the production of this magnificent Grand Tourer.

The story of how the Continental GT came about is as fascinating and complicated as the car itself. The Bentley company, famous for producing some of the fastest and most luxurious English cars money could buy for decades, had been owned by Rolls-Royce, the equally acclaimed aero-engine and car manufacturer, since 1931. But a financial crisis caused by years of inefficiency and a chronic lack of investment led to both Rolls-Royce and Bentley falling into German hands in 1998.

In July of that year, BMW quietly acquired the rights to the Rolls-Royce name (for automotive business) from Rolls-Royce. Days later, Volkswagen bought Rolls-Royce Motor Cars in its entirety, but, as BMW already had the Rolls-Royce name, VW had effectively only purchased Bentley.

It was announced that from midnight, December 31, 2002, Bentley and Rolls-Royce would become separate companies once again, after being together for 67 years . Three months later, VW declared that it was to invest £500 million ($830 million) in Bentley, financing the building of an all-new car.

How this new breed of German-backed Bentley would turn out, no one could tell. Skeptics weren't seriously predicting a 'Golf Continental', but nobody expected quite such a wonderful creation. Its debut at the Paris Motor Show, where a concept model of the new Continental GT was shown for the first

time, caused a sensation, with the full impact of its power and glory being revealed.

The power, 552bhp to be precise, is provided by a six-liter (366 cubic inch) engine with twelve cylinders. But the Volkswagen-built power unit's W12 configuration was a radical departure from Bentleys of the past.

Instead of using two long banks of six cylinders, the W12 staggers the cylinders in each bank, thus effectively creating two narrow-angle V6 engines on a common crankshaft. The result is a phenomenally short engine for its capacity, which frees up precious space. But to match the status of classic Bentleys of old, such as the Continental R of the '50s which was the fastest four-seater on the planet, the new GT needed more muscle than a normally-aspirated, six-liter W12 could provide. The application of two KKK turbochargers sees to that.

With that high-tech power plant driving all four wheels, the Continental GT offers serious supercar performance, while the automatic transmission, operated by paddles mounted under the steering wheel, gives the driver easy access to the power. Want to take a more active part in shifting the Conti along the road? A six-speed manual override is there to do your bidding…

The Bentley's quoted top speed is 198mph, but one car journalist soon reported that, with door mirrors removed and other minor exterior tweaks to reduce drag, a stock Conti R managed 207mph at Volkswagen's high-speed test track in Germany. Acceleration is impressive for a full four-seater car weighing 2,385kg (5,258lb) too, with the 0-60mph

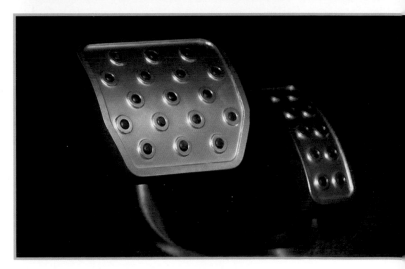

Beautiful Bentley features abound, such as the drilled aluminum brake and accelerator pedals (bottom right)

"Combines cutting edge design, classic craftmanship and the performance of a supercar

sprint taking just 4.7 seconds. Put that performance together with the interior space, offering all the practicality of a four-seater layout, and the result is a vehicle that easily slips onto the role of a regular, everyday form of transport.

You don't even have to be one of the super-rich to own it. Another of the Conti GT's remarkable achievements is its relatively affordable price. When you consider that the company's Continental T of the '90s cost £120,000 ($213,000) more than the GT, the modern car's price looks very good value.

Any fear that the decreased cost of Bentley ownership would be matched by a drop in quality was soon dismissed, too. Those familiar with the Bentley way of doing things will be reassured and comforted by the expanses of top-quality hide and fine wood veneers, while those for whom Bentley ownership is a new experience will discover a new level of luxury, style and effortless good taste. Traditional and unmistakable Bentley touches abound. Perhaps most easily spotted are the classic bulls-eye air vents with their organ stop controls, a feature no Bentley has been without for a generation.

The GT rides on thoroughly modern 19-inch wheels and computer-controlled air suspension, and the chassis features sophisticated electronic traction and stability systems. To haul all this down from high speed the GT's brakes feature the largest diameter discs found on any current production car.

The Continental GT combines cutting-edge design and classic craftsmanship with the performance of a supercar, creating a potent and unique motoring experience. The Bentley boys of the old school would surely approve…. ▨

SPECIFICATION	
ENGINE TYPE	W12 turbocharged
DISPLACEMENT	5,998cc (366 cu in)
POWER	552bhp @ 6,950 rpm
TORQUE	479lb/ft @ 1,600 rpm
TRANSMISSION	Six-speed Tiptronic
0-60mph	4.7 seconds
TOP SPEED	198 mph
PRICE	£112,750 ($159,990)
www.bentleymotors.com	

Acres of leather on the inside and sleek, muscular lines on the outside. The Continental GT is a true Bentley

Bristol
Fighter

" The entire body is designed to control airflow over every surface **"**

It really flies, and no wonder, considering its heritage. The company started off building fighter planes nearly 90 years ago, but this Fighter is a modern-day aerodynamic marvel

There's a reasonable chance you may have never heard of Bristol Cars Limited, but this British company has been crafting exclusive and eccentrically English sports cars since 1946. With strong links to the aircraft industry—the firm was originally part of the Bristol Aeroplane Company—this two-seater car was named after the two-seater Bristol F-2 Fighter airplane that first saw action in World War One over France in 1917.

Today's Fighter is definitely a creation of the modern age, as you can see from the first glance at the pictures on these pages. All that aero industry heritage has paid off in the form of an automobile that cuts through the air more efficiently than any of its competitors. It is the ultimate aerodynamic GT.

There's a big influence from the United States on this very British sporting coupe, the result of a long-term association between Bristol and Chrysler. Bristol's first car, the 407 of 1961, was powered by 5.2 liters (317 cubic inches) of Chrysler V8. The Fighter, which was first unveiled in 2003, also relies on all-American muscle from the same company as its means of high-speed propulsion.

Bristol ships-in engines built for Chrysler's mighty Dodge Viper and tunes the huge 488 cubic-inch (8-liter) V10 to produce 525bhp at 5,600rpm (25bhp more than the Viper SRT-10 of 2003) with a peak torque of 525lb/ft delivered at 3,600 rpm. According to Bristol, the Fighter's horsepower is boosted to 550bhp at high speed due to 'aerodynamic over-pressure' in the inlet system.

They're pretty impressive figures, but customers parting with the Fighter's asking price, the best part of £230,000 ($406,000), appreciate a bit more than brute force. They expect finesse too, and the Fighter

delivers just that, along with outstanding practicality for two-seater capable of over 200mph.

The Fighter is easily the most compact car in its class. Despite the enormous engine, its 1,540kg (3,395lb) curb weight is just 30kg (66lb) more than that of a 2006 Porsche 911 Tiptronic, and the Fighter has a near-perfect weight balance with 48 per cent up front and 52 per cent at the rear. It is fractionally shorter and narrower than the 911 too, having been designed for exceptional agility and steering response, with good manoeuvrability in the city.

Covering the car's steel and aluminum platform chassis are hand-beaten aluminum body panels, with the entire body designed from the outset to control airflow over every surface. Lift and drag has been optimized, even though aerodynamic aids such

Bristol has had a special relationship with Chrysler for decades, using the American company's engines to power many of its models. The Fighter uses a tuned version of the Dodge Viper's huge V10 power plant for motive power

The interior of the Fighter is eccentrically English. Driver's eye view (see top of previous page) reflects Bristol's history, giving the impression of a fighter-plane cockpit

as wings, splitters or venturi do not feature.

The Fighter's carbon-fiber gullwing doors give unobstructed entry with a gracious exit, even in confined spaces. The well-appointed interior has practical luggage space and will suit drivers from 5' to 6' 7" in height. A full-size spare wheel/tire is fitted and the Fighter also has generous ground clearance.

For those who like to travel places fast, and with as little time spent at the gas station as possible, the Fighter's fuel capacity is a real boon. The standard 100-liter (26.4 US gallon) gas tank can be boosted to an optional 135-liter (35.7 US gallons) capacity, giving a range of between 425 and 650 miles. The suspension system features double wishbones at front and rear, with big ventilated discs squeezed by six-piston front and four-piston rear calipers dealing with slowing things down.

For some people, though, too much is just not enough, and in mid-2005 Bristol decided to offer the Fighter with a little bit more. Particularly power-hungry, speed-starved customers could order the new Fighter S. With a reworked, re-tuned V10, the 'S' version pumps out a massive 628bhp (increasing to 650bhp with 'aerodynamic overpressure') and 580ft/lb of torque. To that they can also add the 'R' pack with 19" wheels, sharpened steering response, lowered ride height and sportier suspension. And to that they can also add the 'C' (competition) pack with an even lower ride height, competition-style fuel fillers and aerodynamic aids which lower the car's drag coefficient to 0.255 – a figure which Bristol claims is the lowest of any production car.

Bearing in mind that the company's claimed top speed for the base-model Fighter is 'approximately 210mph', they surely need to rename the 'SRC' version the 'Jet Fighter'!

SPECIFICATION	
ENGINE TYPE	V10
DISPLACEMENT	7,996cc (488 cu in)
POWER	628bhp (increasing to 660bhp at high speed)
TORQUE	580lb/ft @ 3,900rpm
TRANSMISSION	Six-speed manual (optional four-speed auto)
0-60mph	3.9 seconds approx
TOP SPEED	215mph approx
PRICE	£256,150 ($452,540 approx)
www.bristolcars.co.uk	

The Bristol's carbon-fiber gullwing doors give unobstructed entry with a graceful exit. This practicality also extends to surprisingly good luggage space, accessed by the rear hatchback

Brabus SLR

The most extreme version of the Mercedes-Benz SLR McLaren, the Brabus SLR packs high-tech performance

The Brabus SLR is an intimidating piece of machinery. The side-exit pipes (above) echo the SLR racers of the '50s and allow the underbody to be aerodynamically smooth

The Mercedes-Benz SLR McLaren is an impressive piece of auto engineering. With a supercharged 5,439cc (332 cubic inch) V8, swing-wing doors, carbon-fiber bodywork and a catalog of other cutting-edge technology, it's a true 21st-century GT.

The 'Merclaren' SLR builds on the legacy of the famous Mercedes SLR factory race cars of the '50s, 'open' sports racers that could nudge 190mph on a long straight. The modern-day SLR tops that, with a maximum speed of 208mph from its 585bhp engine. It can also catapult this car from zero to 62mph in 3.8 seconds, to 124mph in 10.6, and on to 186mph in 28.8 on the way to its upper limit.

Helping it to hit that horsepower, the newly-developed SLR engine has a compact, twin-screw supercharger installed between the two cylinder banks that spins at up to 23,000rpm at a pressure of 0.9 bar. The power unit also delivers serious low-down punch, with 442lb/ft of torque at just 1,500rpm and peak torque of 575lb/ft arriving at 3,250rpm.

Mounted low down on a strong aluminum frame, the engine features three valves per cylinder, dry sump lubrication and four catalytic converters. Each SLR engine is individually built by hand, with one hand-picked Mercedes craftsman carrying out the entire process. The five-speed auto transmission has

a manual program with three shift stages—Sport, SuperSport and Race—which progressively shorten shift times, with the driver able to change ratios by buttons on the steering wheel or via the stick.

But it's the SLR's braking system that stands out as this car's technological highlight. The eight-piston front calipers bite on discs made from a carbon-fiber-reinforced ceramic material. These generate deceleration of up to 1.3g, have power equivalent to 2,000bhp and can handle temperatures of up to 1,000° C (1,832° F).

These brake discs not only offer a level of fade-resistance not previously achieved in a production car, but also weigh 60 per cent less than regular discs. They don't corrode either, and have a service life of nearly 200,000 miles. And if that's not enough, there's also an airbrake. Step heavily on the brake

pedal and the rear spoiler rises to an angle of 65 degrees, boosting braking by increasing drag.

There's a historical resonance here, as effective airbrakes were a revolutionary feature of the SLRs raced at Le Mans in 1955. In common with those old SLR racers, the modern SLR also has large-diameter

> " The dash, center console and door panels are made from carbon fiber "

Brabus created its own interior for the SLR, using red leather and Alcantara and an elaborately-stitched leather floor. The flat-bottomed steering wheel has gearshift buttons in the spokes

stainless steel exhausts which exit (now on both sides) from just behind the front wheels. Having the pipes at the side allows the car to have a smooth underbody, which plays a crucial role in producing excellent aerodynamics. They also give voice to the SLR's very satisfying V8 bark.

The swing-wing doors are a distinctive feature adopted from another historic Mercedes of 1955, the SLR Coupe. Just two examples of this beautiful hard-top, essentially a factory W196 racer with a roof, were built, on the instruction of Mercedes' Competition Director Rudi Uhlenhaut. He used them as personal transport, mainly to whisk himself to and from race circuits all over Europe. These 176mph coupes were never put into volume production and Uhlenhaut's unique pair of high-speed runarounds were never sold.

The SLR Coupe's doors were attached to the roof itself, but on today's SLR they are attached to the A-pillar. The modern car also features up-to-the-minute driver's aids like Sensotronic Brake Control, Electronic Stability Program and tire-pressure

monitoring, along with 18" wheels and suspension components crafted from lightweight aluminum.

But for those who want even more, and have the extra £98,000 ($176,000) or so to pay for it, there's the Brabus Sport Program for the SLR. This package features a special self-locking differential, further optimizing the super sports car's traction, further improving acceleration. The engine has improved fuel cooling, custom camshafts and open (not for street use) exhausts, which boost power from 585 to 652bhp. This shaves two-tenths from the 0-62mph time and adds 3mph to the SLR's top speed.

To reduce lift on the front axle and improve high-speed directional stability, Brabus also fits a new spoiler on the front air dam, while the stock, ten-spoke 18" wheels are uprated with the use of multi-piece 20" six-spokers shod with 255/30 and 305/25 ZR 20 tires.

Brabus' own upholstery shop created a revised interior with a combination of black and red leather and Alcantara. The 'waffle-design' stitching of the leather floor is especially elaborate and requires

7,800 meters (25,591 feet) of the finest thread in its creation. Then there's the Brabus flat-bottomed sports steering wheel with gearshift buttons in the spokes and, finally, the dashboard, center console and door panels are all made from precisely-fitting exposed carbon pieces.

Well, if your neighbors all drove SLRs, wouldn't you want the Brabus version? ✕

SPECIFICATION	
ENGINE TYPE	V8 supercharged
DISPLACEMENT	5,439cc (332 cu in)
POWER	652bhp @ 6,500rpm
TORQUE	n/a (stock SLR: 575lb/ft @ 3,250-5,000rpm)
TRANSMISSION	Five-speed auto with 'Speedshift'
0-60mph	3.6 seconds
TOP SPEED	211mph
PRICE	€600,000 (£411,600 or $737,640 approx)
www.brabus.com	

This is the starting point for every Brabus SLR. The German company modifies a Mercedes-Benz SLR McLaren like the one above, taking it to even greater extremes of performance

Convertibles

Convertible: A stylish two-door car without a fixed roof. Instead, the roof folds away or is otherwise removed so that the passenger compartment is exposed to the open air

Lamborghini Murciélago Roadster

Ferrari Superamerica

Porsche Carrera GT

Bentley Azure

" The latest in a long line of highly desirable "
Bentley 'dropheads' which go
back many decades

Bentley Azure

Whether it's cruising around high-class areas like Beverly Hills or London's Mayfair, the Azure can't be beaten for pure impact. Effortless style and speed are its hallmarks

For the ultimate in open-topped comfort and luxury, there's really nothing on the market today to match the fabulous Bentley Azure. The new Azure is the latest in a long line of highly desirable Bentley 'dropheads' which go back many decades in the history of the marque.

It was the glamorous Arnage Drophead Coupe show car that appeared at the Los Angeles Auto Show in January 2005 which showed what was to come. When the Azure emerged as a production model, its specification was virtually unchanged from that show car. The only modifications amounted to the fitting of carbon-fiber underfloor cross-braces for added body stiffness and some relatively minor adjustments to the body trim.

The Azure shares its front-end styling with the current Arnage range and its large body size ensures supreme comfort for four adults. The interior is newly designed, with a stunning bespoke interior, while the complex folding of the intricate three-layer fabric roof is operated hydraulically at the touch of a switch. The whole roof assembly stows gracefully beneath the hide-trimmed tonneau in less than thirty seconds.

This latest Azure was unveiled at the Frankfurt Motor Show in September 2005, with the previous model's seven-year production run having ended in 2002. The old car's 6.75-liter (412 cubic inch) twin-turbocharged V8 engine produced a healthy 400bhp

Touches of luxury abound in the Azure. Beautiful walnut adorns the dashboard (above) while the superbly-tooled leather back seat is just as tempting as the driver's seat

at 4,100rpm with 616lb/ft of torque at 2,150rpm, endowing it with a 0-60mph time of 6.3 seconds and a top speed of 155mph.

The 2006 Azure makes an even more athletic 450bhp at the same revs, and 645lb/ft at 3,250rpm and although its 0-60 acceleration remains the same, the new car can now reach an unrestricted 168mph.

The 17-inch wheels of the previous Azure have been upgraded to 19-inch items, along with bigger brake discs all round. Although external changes are subtle, the latest version has a slightly longer wheelbase than before, along with a wider track and a longer body with a taller roof. The new Azure's steering is slightly quicker than the old model, too.

On the subject of old models, the history of Bentley open tourers goes back over a total of nine decades. The first Bentleys ever built were open cars powered by a four-cylinder '3 Liter' engine. The second of these, first exhibited in London in 1919, featured a cylinder head with four valves for each cylinder—something which didn't become common on production cars until eight decades later.

Bentley enjoyed early success at the Le Mans 24 hour race (its team cars scoring five victories from 1924-1930) despite being described by rival maker Ettore Bugatti as "the fastest lorries in the world".

However, after the company was acquired by Rolls-Royce in 1931, the character of Bentleys soon became much more refined and they became widely known as 'silent sports cars'. In more recent times there has rarely been a time when a convertible Bentley has not been in production, with some of the more famous being the S series Continental dropheads of the 1950s and '60s and the T series Corniche of the '70s and '80s.

Today's Azure is fundamentally a much improved version of the Continental S convertible first seen at the Geneva Motor show in 1995. But, just as in decades past, if a prospective Bentley Azure owner has specific requirements which the standard listed models cannot satisfy, Bentley Motors stands ready and able to carry out a wide variety of personal modifications to the body, interior, engine or chassis to ensure that the customer receives precisely the motor of his or her dreams. ▨

SPECIFICATION	
ENGINE TYPE	V8, twin turbo
DISPLACEMENT	6,761cc (412 cu in)
POWER	450bhp @ 4,100rpm
TORQUE	645lb/ft @ 3,250rpm
TRANSMISSION	Four-speed auto
0-60 mph	5.9 seconds
TOP SPEED	168mph
PRICE	£222,500 ($329,990)
www.bentleymotors.com	

This drophead Bentley's cabin offers opulence without parallel. The whole roof assembly stows gracefully under the hide-trimmed tonneau in less than thirty seconds

" One of the most exotic and exclusive automobiles on the road "

Ferrari Superamerica

Ferraris are renowned for their sheer sex appeal, but the Superamerica is a convertible with a unique attraction. Its rotating electronic roof is nearly as rapid as the car itself

There are some very fast cars that offer open-top motoring, but Ferrari's limited edition 199mph Superamerica is currently the fastest true, touch-of-a-button convertible. It is also the only one with a Revocromico roof, a clever device that electrically rotates through 180 degrees in less than 10 seconds to open or close.

When open, the roof lies flush with the trunk lid. It's made from around a square meter (just over a square yard) of shaped electrochromic glass which changes the density of its tint via a five-position switch on the center tunnel. The lightest setting is similar to a conventional glass roof's, but within 60 seconds this can be altered to block out 99 per cent of sunlight; it automatically returns to this setting when the engine is off, to protect the interior.

The Revocromico design provides other benefits, too. The carbon-fiber support buttresses serve as robust roll-over protection, while rear trunk access and space is unaffected whether the roof is open or closed. When in the open position, the heated rear screen remains in place to double as an effective wind deflector. There is even a tonneau cover to protect the glass when in the open position, but if this isn't fitted, and it rains, Superamerica occupants could suffer a wet roof on the inside when it's closed again. Not that they'll be particularly concerned, as the Superamerica has plenty of other distractions.

Ferrari fans will know that the Superamerica is basically a convertible version of the hardtop 575M.

Underneath the skin, structural reinforcements are in place to compensate for the unstressed glass roof, but on the outside it's pretty much the same car from the nose to the A-pillar.

The engine is the same configuration as the 575M, an all-aluminum-alloy 65 degree V12 with four overhead cams, 48 valves and dry sump lubrication. However, due to higher-flow intake tracts, manifold and inlet ducts, along with a new exhaust system with reduced back pressure, the Superamerica's

The Superamerica has the same basic engine as its Ferrari stablemate, the 575M, but its 552bhp power output is greater thanks to the addition of tuning parts

engine makes a healthy 532bhp at 7,250rpm, making it 25bhp more powerful than the 575's.

Both the 575 and Superamerica have a rear-mounted transaxle with a six-speed transmission, operated either by a conventional manual stick or, on the F1-style gearbox, sequentially using paddles mounted just behind the steering wheel.

With the paddle-change set-up, the Superamerica accelerates slightly harder than the version with manual transmission, hitting 60mph from zero in 4.2 seconds due to the quicker gearshifting. The high-tech box of tricks can shift a gear in 180 milliseconds when in Sport setting. The F1A transmission can also be set in auto mode.

A GTC handling pack can also be fitted to the Superamerica, including sportier suspension (stiffer springs and anti-roll bar), a sports exhaust and hugely effective carbon composite brake discs developed in collaboration with top manufacturer Brembo.

With styling by Pininfarina, today's Superamerica is named after a series of very exclusive models built by Ferrari in the late 1950s and early '60s. The first of these was the 410 Superamerica of 1956. These V12-powered cars wore stunning coachwork in both coupe and convertible styles. In fact, no two 410 Superamericas were alike, and the roster of owners included royalty and captains of industry from the US and Europe.

Back in those days, Ferrari's Maranello factory turned out these limited-production specials at the rate of about one every month, so specific customer requirements and major customizations were not only possible but positively encouraged.

Fortunately, these days the Carrozzeria Scaglietti Personalization Program also allows customers to specify additional styling, equipment and functional options for the Superamerica, if not quite to the extremes of yesteryear. In any specification, though, a convertible Superamerica remains one of the most exotic and exclusive automobiles on the road. ✄

SPECIFICATION	
ENGINE TYPE	V12
DISPLACEMENT	5,748cc (350.8 cu in)
POWER	532bhp @ 7,250rpm
TORQUE	434lb/ft @ 5,250rpm
TRANSMISSION	Six-speed sequential 'F1A' or manual
0-62mph	4.20 seconds (F1A), 4.25 seconds (manual)
TOP SPEED	199mph
PRICE	£191,000 ($305,000)
www.ferrariworld.com	

This Ferrari's Revocromico electronic roof makes it an exotic and practical convertible. In the case of unexpected showers, it can be closed effortlessly in ten seconds flat

" The Murciélago makes one of the most sensuous sounds in motoring "

Lamborghini
Murciélago Roadster

To enjoy the full effect of the Murciélago's sensual engine note, the open-topped version is the one. Backed up with its awesome road presence, it gives serious sensory overload

Maybe Lamborghini's stunning Murciélago Roadster shouldn't be included here, at least not in the Convertibles section. Some might say it's really an open car and not a true convertible, even though it comes with what the company describes as an 'R-top' roof.

Those skeptics should follow these instructions. First, look at the definition of convertible on page 29: basically 'a stylish two-door car without a fixed roof'. Then take a longer look at the photographs of the Murciélago on these pages. Only a person who is not in full command of their senses would argue against the inclusion of this bullish 572bhp Roadster here, and it is welcomed with open arms.

Getting back to the subject of the Murciélago's roof, the R-top is a soft covering only intended for temporary use, for protection from the elements during sudden, unexpected rain showers. When the roof is in use, Lamborghini recommends that the driver limits speed to a maximum of only 100mph, 99mph slower than the car's claimed top speed when the roof is stowed away.

First presented as a concept car in January 2003 at the Detroit Auto Show, the production Murciélago Roadster made its official debut at the Geneva Show the following year. Fortunately for Lamborghini, this Roadster has already proved more successful than some of the its earlier convertibles.

Lamborghini's first convertible was the 1965 350 GTS. Powered by an in-house 3.5-liter V12 engine

with 320bhp, this glamorous two-seater 'spyder' had coachwork by Touring, could dash to 60mph in well under seven seconds and reach 155mph. Sadly, just two examples were built.

Then followed the exquisite Miura Roadster, with its mid-mounted 4-liter V12 engine. Designed by Marcello Gandini with bodywork by Bertone, it was first seen at the Brussels Show in 1968. Like the more recent Murciélago Roadster at Detroit, the open Miura was a real show-stopper.

Unfortunately, this 174mph beauty did not manage to attract enough buyers to progress it from show prototype to a production model. Perhaps because of this disappointment, as well as Lamborghini's on-going financial turmoil and the technical difficulties involved in producing an open-top car, a Countach Roadster was never attempted.

The company's successful return to the world of wind-in-the-hair motoring came with the Gandini-designed Diablo Roadster of 1996-2000. The standard car's 5.7-liter V12 made 492bhp and it was claimed it could top 200mph. In 1998 the Diablo Roadster SV was added. This even more exotic version punched out a fulsome 530 horsepower and, in this author's opinion, sounds better than any road car before or since. The SV could also sprint to 60mph

With intense loads put on the car's structure by the big V12's power, some areas have to be beefed up. Serious cross-bracing keeps the engine bay stiffened up (right)

The Murciélago Roadster retains one of Lamborghini's most distinctive features: doors which swing upwards rather than outwards when they are opened

in 3.6 seconds and contributed to the Sant 'Agata factory's tally of 468 Diablo Roadsters built.

Unlike some Lamborghini roadsters of the past, the Murciélago's modifications go further than the removal of the roof panel. The whole of the car above its waistline, from the windshield back, is new. The glass parts have been designed like a crash-helmet visor, to integrate smoothly with the body's exterior lines. So the aesthetics and aerodynamics of the car aren't disturbed, the electronically-controlled roll-over bars extend only when necessary. The new 18-inch wheels (13" wide at the rear) mesh with traditional Lamborghini design, with round holes intersecting the spokes. The six-speed manual transmission can be had with standard or close ratios and, as an option, with the sequential, paddle-shift 'E gear' system.

Like its Diablo predecessor, the Murciélago is also equipped with a permanent four-wheel-drive system with limited-slip differentials at the front and rear. This acts as an active traction control system,

with excess torque at the rear wheels automatically transferred to the front. In addition, there is also an electronic traction-control system.

Some of the car's structural components have been redesigned to ensure torsional stiffness, while the suspension is independent at the front with double wishbones at the rear. The anti-roll bars have 'antidive' and 'antisquat' systems. Self-adjusting Koni shock absorbers are used, and the braking system has big Brembo calipers acting on ventilated discs.

The Roadster's exhaust pipes are also new, with a bigger bore than the hardtop's. Through these, the Murciélago gives voice to one of the most sensuous sounds in motoring world, and in the Roadster the driver can revel in this without the sound-deadening effect of a metal roof. Of course, to experience this aural accompaniment to the absolute full, a driver has to be prepared to rev the motor hard through the gears and then cope with the vast speeds that result. Fortunately, traction is strong, as are the

brakes, and as long as the driver maintains a firm grip on everything, including the steering wheel and gearstick, this Lamborghini can gives a whole new meaning to the word 'joyride'.

Maybe the Murciélago Roadster is not a true convertible in the strictest sense, but it is certainly brutishly powerful and incredibly exhilarating. So if you live somewhere warm and sunny, who cares?

SPECIFICATION	
ENGINE TYPE	V12
DISPLACEMENT	6,192cc (378 cu in)
POWER	572bhp @ 7,500rpm
TORQUE	479lb/ft @ 5,400rpm
TRANSMISSION	Six-speed manual
0-60mph	3.8 seconds
TOP SPEED	199mph
PRICE	£223,250 ($319,250)
www.lamborghini.com	

"No Le Mans driver hammering along at 200mph ever enjoyed this kind of luxury"

Porsche Carrera GT

Manufacturers often make claims that their cars feature racing technology, but Porsche can truly say that about the Carrera GT—it's a road-going racer with added refinement

Porsche's ultimate auto, the Carrera GT, did not have to be here along with the other convertibles. With 'GT' in its name, it could have slotted in with the other GTs featured earlier in this book. And its power and performance stats: 608bhp, a 0-60mph time of 3.8 seconds, a standing quarter-mile time of 11.4 seconds and a top speed of 205mph would justify a placing with the European supercars described later. But a convertible it is, for when the sun shines, this supercar GT has a light-weight detachable hardtop that is easily removed and stowed in the luggage compartment.

Porsche says the Carrera GT was conceived during the 24 Hours of Le Mans in 1998, the year when the company secured its sixteenth outright victory. The idea was proposed for a road-going sports car based exclusively on racing technology, and two years later, in the autumn of 2000, the whole project began to take shape.

That 1998 race was won by a Porsche GT1, a car that had gone on sale in road-legal guise for the best part of $1m in the previous year, to make the GT1 racers eligible for race regulations. The GT1 was basically a very hi-tech, lightweight 911 coupe with a bodystyle that looked like it had melted slightly and powered by a twin-turbocharged 3.2-liter flat six making 544bhp.

The 1,380kg (3,042lb) Carrera GT turned out to be 130kg (286lb) heavier than the road-going GT1, but these two cars have virtually identical

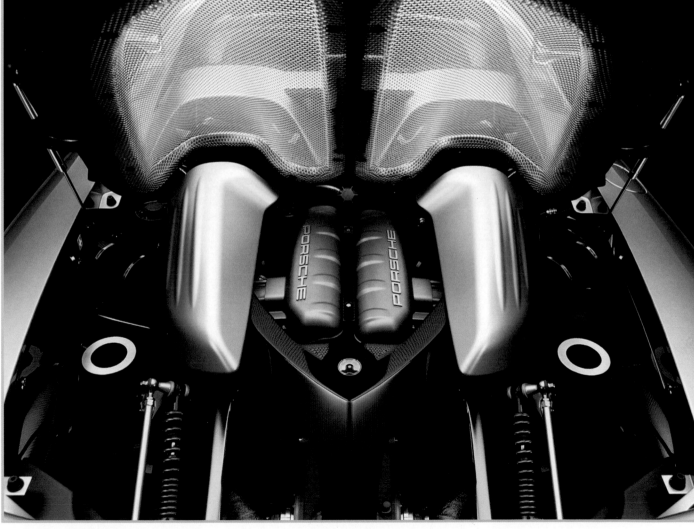

The Carrera GT's 5.7-liter V10 was originally developed as a race engine, but never actually saw competitive action on the track

performance: a road-spec GT1 can do 0-60 in 3.6 seconds, the standing quarter-mile in 11.6 and reach a maximum speed of 206mph.

So, the order of things as the story unfolded went like this: 1). Porsche builds a GT1 race car to win Le Mans. 2). Porsche builds 'homologation' GT1 road cars. 3). Porsche wins Le Mans. 4). Porsche builds the Carrera GT using race technology and takes it to market in September 2003.

The Carrera GT borrows some technology from the winning GT1, but it's no carbon copy. The road car is powered not by the latter's flat-six turbo, but by a mid-mounted, normally-aspirated 5.7-liter V10. This is an evolution of a 5.5-liter race engine that was being developed until Porsche pulled the plug and the program was cancelled. The GT's 10 cylinders are arranged in a 68° 'V', its crankshaft is forged and its con rods are fashioned from titanium. Its four-valve heads have sodium-cooled exhaust valves and its intake cams feature Porsche's Vario-Cam system, using a rotary adjuster for continuous regulation and adjustment of camshaft phase angle.

In addition to its 612bhp, this engine makes 435lb/ft of torque at 5,750rpm and revs to 8,400rpm. All this is fed via a dry, two-plate 'ceramic composite' clutch, which is 10 times lighter than a conventional clutch, to a special race-specification, transversely-mounted six-speed manual gearbox. The chassis is made from aerospace-grade composites, including carbon-fiber sandwich construction with a high-strength honeycomb core.

The technology that the Carrera GT inherited from the 911 GT1 race car includes the suspension system. This is a double-wishbone arrangement (aerodynamically refined at the rear) with inboard springs and dampers. In contrast to a regular road car set-up, each spring-and-damper unit—plus the corresponding anti-roll bar—is actuated using a pushrod and rocker.

The GT's ultra-lightweight wheels (19" front, 20" rear) are made from forged magnesium rather than the regular aluminum alloy. Its tires have an integrated pressure-monitoring system and the brakes feature ventilated, cross-drilled 380mm (15") ceramic composite discs.

The festival of GT technology continues inside: the trip computer display features high-resolution dot-matrix technology, the door windows have a

'hydrophobic' coating which helps disperse water to provide a clearer view of the mirrors, while the leather-upholstered seats have a single-piece carbon-fiber and Kevlar shell. But the GT isn't purely about high-tech and high speed.

The aluminum gearshift has a natural wood inlay in homage to the first Porsche to claim an outright victory at Le Mans, the 917 of 1971, which had a balsa wood gearknob fitted with as a last-minute measure to reduce weight. What's more, the GT's luggage compartment has two tailored travel bags, a briefcase, shoulder bag and centre console bag, all made from leather matched to the interior of the car. Other no-cost options include satellite navigation and a BOSE audio system with Active Equalization and a pair of 100-watt amps driving six speakers.

No Le Mans driver hammering along at over 200mph ever enjoyed that kind of luxury. ✉

SPECIFICATION	
ENGINE TYPE	V10
DISPLACEMENT	5,733cc (350 cu in)
POWER	612bhp @ 8,000rpm
TORQUE	435lb/ft @ 5,750rpm
TRANSMISSION	Six-speed manual
0-60mph	3.8 seconds
TOP SPEED	205mph
PRICE	€461,058 (£313,400 or $550,000 approx)
www.porsche.com	

Functional but luxurious, the GT's cabin is pure quality. Below: the view other drivers will see of this fearsomely quick Porsche—a rapidly disappearing back end!

Euro Supercars

A two-seater car designed and/or manufactured in Europe with striking appearance, surplus horsepower and extreme dynamic performance, acceleration and top speed.

Bugatti Veyron

Ferrari FXX

Koenigsegg CCR

Maserati MC12

Pagani Zonda F

" So awesomely fast it has no road-going rivals to challenge it "

Bugatti Veyron

It is the most expensive production car in the world. It is also the fastest, and that's official. The Veyron is the Everest of engineering and the pinnacle of road car performance

If this book was called 'Ultimate Auto' and featured just one car, Bugatti's incredible Veyron would have to be it, for all sorts of reasons. So let's take a look at what makes it so special...

First, the Veyron is the most expensive production car on sale today. At over one million euros (around $1.4m or £800,000) it is not the most expensive new car ever (that accolade goes to the late '90s Mercedes-Benz CLK-GTR which in the UK sold for £1,175,000, the equivalent of $1.9 million) but it is a whole heap more than every other new car.

Second, although the 987bhp Veyron isn't quite the most powerful car on paper (see the 1,046bhp SSC Ultimate Aero featured later in this book), it is the fastest. In May 2005 at VW's Ehra proving ground in Germany, the Veyron was independently timed at 248.5mph by the German homologation authority (TUV), and it achieved this speed several times running in both directions, as required by the TUV. This beat the Koenigsegg CCR's 241mph world record set three months earlier. What's more, Bugatti's quoted top speed for the Veyron is 253mph, electronically limited for tire safety reasons.

Third, the Veyron's sixteen-cylinder motor is the most impressive engine that has ever been squeezed into a production car. The car world has witnessed sixteen-cylinder power units before: Cadillac's 1930s V16 Fleetwood and its recent 'Sixteen' concept car

are two, along with the little-known early 1930s Marmon and the 1930 Bugatti Type 47 Grand Sport, but none of these had its cylinders arranged in a 'W' configuration. Neither did they have four turbos, or as many as 64 valves and 10 radiators, or a titanium exhaust system, all of which combine to produce the Veyron's massive 922lb/ft of torque. In common with all Volkswagen Group engines, the Bugatti's power was measured at a stifling 40°C (104°F). In more moderate temperatures of around 20°C (68°F) power increases to around 1,035bhp.

The Veyron's chassis is a carbon-fiber tub design, and most of the body is made from carbon-fiber with some aluminum panels. Only carbon-ceramic brake discs would do for this car, and they can bring it to rest from its top speed in under 10 seconds. Its 20-inch tires are specially-developed Michelin PAX run-flats, which require special wheels and are the most sophisticated automotive tires available. The rears, at 365 millimeters (14 inches) across, are the widest ever fitted to a road car and its transmission is a seven-speed, twin-clutch DSG semi-automatic sequential that feeds power to all four wheels.

Despite its substantial 1,950kg (4,300lb) weight

The Veyron's incredible W16 engine (top); the rear wing gives much-needed aerodynamic downforce (center); center console is in beautifully machined aluminum

when fully fuelled up and ready to go, the Veyron's acceleration is on a par with a grand prix racing car: 0-60mph in 2.46 seconds and 0-100mph in under five seconds. It has so much power and grip it can rocket from zero to 200mph in exactly the same time it took the McLaren F1 to accelerate from 135mph to 200mph.

Quite simply, the Bugatti Veyron is so awesomely fast it has no road-going rivals that can challenge it on performance, at least not in a straight line.

Bugatti's reputation was built during the 1920s and '30s with a series of feisty little sports racers and Grand Tourers, but the Veyron is not the first outrageous Bugatti to stun the car world.

In the early 1930s the company built just six Type 41 Royales. With a massive 12,763cc (778cu in) 300 horsepower straight-eight engine and the most extravagant coachwork bolted to an enormous chassis running on 24-inch wheels, the Royale was (and still is) the pinnacle of automotive excess. All six Royales survive to this day, and were displayed at the Pebble Beach Concours d'Elegance in 1985.

By the mid-1950s, Bugatti had passed its prime and the company dissolved. Then, in the late '80s, Bugatti was resurrected and produced the four-wheel-drive EB110 supercar with a four-turbo, 3.5-litre V12 which, by 1994, was producing a healthy 603bhp in 'GT' guise.

In 1998 the Volkswagen Group acquired the rights to Bugatti and the Veyron story began. The first show concept under VW ownership was the 18-cylinder EB118 grand tourer. This was followed by the EB218, the 18/3 Chiron and the EB Veyron 18.4. Then the Veyron 16.4 concept followed in 2000 and, following an extended period of development, the production Veyron finally hit the streets in late 2005. High-speed stability and engine cooling issues delayed first deliveries for at least two years past the original stated on-sale date.

The end result is a super-luxury hypercar which, in many ways, eclipses all other supercars... and almost upstages its legendary Royale ancestor.

SPECIFICATION	
ENGINE TYPE	W16 turbo
DISPLACEMENT	7,993cc (487.6 cu in)
POWER	987bhp @ 6,000rpm
TORQUE	922lb/ft @ 2,200-5,500rpm
TRANSMISSION	Seven-speed DSG sequential
0-62mph	2.46 seconds
TOP SPEED	253mph (limited)
PRICE	€1,160,000 (£800,000, $1,412,000 approx) plus local taxes

www.bugatti-cars.de/bugatti/

The Veyron's special tires are the most sophisticated on the market, but its incredible power gets them smokin' easily (left). Inside, it's full Bugatti luxury (below)

Ferrari
FXX

To own an FXX, you have to be a Ferrari VIP, and you get more than a car for the $1.8 million price tag…

The Bugatti Veyron is described on the previous pages as the most expensive car in the world, but it won't take a genius to calculate that this $1.8 million Ferrari FXX costs the best part of half a million dollars more than the Veyron. The difference is that when purchasing an FXX, the customer is buying into more than just ownership of the car.

With the FXX, your $1.8 million also gives you Ferrari 'Client Test Driver' status. This is a package which includes participation in a series of Ferrari-organized track events on various international-level circuits in Europe, North America and Japan. You get the benefit of a Ferrari 'pit crew' too, with factory technicians on hand to provide any assistance and support required by the Client Test Drivers. FXX owners can also take their cars out on the track independently during private sessions, and should they choose to leave their car at Ferrari's Maranello HQ when they are not in use, Ferrari will transport their FXX to the various European circuits for the scheduled events.

The FXX is the culmination of a series of low-volume production 'extreme sports' Ferraris, which in the modern mid-engined era began with the 1984 288 GTO. This stripped-out lightweight had a 400bhp twin-turbo V8 and could nudge 190mph. This was followed in 1987 by the 201mph F40 with its 478bhp twin-turbocharged V8, and in 1995 by the F50. With

The FXX's power is provided by the V12 engine from Ferrari's Enzo supercar. Naturally, as this is an extravagant track toy for the privileged few, its capacity is even larger than the Enzo's and it produces even more power, with over 800bhp

"The package includes participation in a series of Ferrari-organized track events"

a 513bhp V12 engine derived directly from Ferrari's 1990 single-seat grand prix racer, the 207mph F50 was the first car to bring genuine Formula One technology to the road.

In 1996 Ferrari quietly produced a very small number of FX models. Based on the flat-12-engined F512M, the FX featured heavily restyled bodywork and a Williams-BMW-developed sequential gearbox. Although at least one FX found its way into private hands, it never went on sale to the general public.

Then in 2003 came the Enzo, on which the FXX is based. This car has a carbon-fiber and aluminum honeycomb chassis, very advanced aerodynamics and a 5,998cc (366 cubic inch) V12 producing 660bhp at 7,800rpm and 484lb/ft of torque at 5,500rpm. Assisted by a sequential transmission able to change gears in as little as 150 milliseconds, it could manage 0-62mph in 3.65 seconds, 0-124mph in 9.5 seconds, 0-124-0mph in just 14.2 seconds and a 217.5mph top speed. Tipping the scales at 1,365kg (3,009lb) and selling at around £425,000 ($640,000), the Enzo was Ferrari's ultimate supercar.

Then, at the 2005 Bologna Motor Show, the FXX made its debut. As it has not been certified for road or race use, the FXX is an extravagant track toy for those who don't have the time or the inclination for real racing, but who are sensible enough to realize that the public road is not the best place to exploit their cars' full potential.

Powered by an enlarged 6,262cc (382 cubic inch) Enzo V12 it develops over 800 horsepower at 8500 rpm and the improved sequential gearbox delivers gear changes in under 100 milliseconds—almost as fast as Ferrari's current Formula One grand prix cars. Bridgestone developed a 19-inch slick tire specifically for the FXX, while Brembo created a special brake pad and cooling system for the composite ceramic material discs.

Another unique feature is the car's sophisticated telemetry system, which monitors and provides feedback in real time, while the Magneti Marelli instrument panel incorporates a new data acquisition system. A rear-facing video camera is installed on the FXX's roof which, combined with a special display on the dash, means rear-view mirrors are not necessary, thereby improving aerodynamics.

With a dry weight of 1,155kg (2,546lb) the FXX can do a lap of Ferrari's Fiorano test track in under

1 minute 18 seconds. Although those special slick tires give it a very big advantage, the FXX puts all other Ferrari models' lap times in the shade (F40: 1m 31.5s; F50: 1m 28.0s; Enzo: 1m 25.3s). Yes, the FXX is over seven seconds a lap faster than the blisteringly quick Enzo.

Given the car's exceptional performance and the unique nature of the package, not to mention the substantial cost involved, delivery of each FXX also includes an advanced driving course with tuition provided by the best professional drivers. Courses take place at the Fiorano Circuit, where Ferrari carries out testing on its Formula One racing cars. After the pedals have been set and seat individually molded for each driver, there follows a traditional shakedown test and then a training session.

Apart from the huge expense, becoming an FXX Client Test Driver isn't easy. All potential candidates must first be vetted and approved by an in-house Ferrari committee. And sorry to break this news to you, but only 29 cars have been built, and yes, you guessed it, every one is spoken for. ▨

SPECIFICATION	
ENGINE TYPE	V12
DISPLACEMENT	6,262cc (382 cu in)
POWER	800+bhp @ 8,500rpm
TORQUE	508lb/ft
TRANSMISSION	Six-speed sequential manual
0-62mph	n/a (Enzo 3.65 seconds)
TOP SPEED	n/a (Enzo 217.5mph)
PRICE	€1,500,000 (approx $1,800,000, £1,020,000) plus local taxes
www.ferrariworld.com	

A feast of carbon-fiber greets the driver in the cockpit of the FXX. As a great deal of the car is made from this incredibly light and strong material, why not show it off?

Koenigsegg CCX

It's pronounced Kur-nig-segg. You may never have heard of this car company, but one of its previous models was a world record holder. The CCX is the latest of the breed

In February 2005, a small team from Sweden gathered at the Nardo proving ground in Italy with their completely stock Koenigsegg CCR. Their mission was to break the production road car speed record, which at the time was held by the awesome McLaren F1 at 240.3mph.

The CCR's 806bhp should have whipped the McLaren's 627bhp, but things are rarely that simple. One handicap for the Swedes was that the McLaren's record was achieved at VW's Ehra proving ground in Germany, which features a 5.6-mile-long straight. The Nardo track is a 7.8-mile circle, which means that at high speed the car is constantly turning. The extra friction caused by this turning saps precious horsepower and scrubs off speed.

The car accelerated onto the track and recorded a speed of 241.02mph. Though only 0.72mph faster than the McLaren, that was enough to grab the record. The Koenigsegg crew had to be satisfied with the fact that when the McLaren had been run at Nardo it recorded 231.2mph, while a Ferrari Enzo had managed only 220.6mph.

But, as the saying goes, it's tough at the top. Just three months later, Bugatti showed up at Ehra and its Veyron went 248.5mph. Despite that, whichever way you look at it, the Koenigsegg CCR is fast, but what exactly is a Koenigsegg?

The project started in 1994 with the concept of building a high-tech, two-seat supercar. A working

prototype was built by the end of the following year, and much of 1996 was spent testing and developing on the track, on the highway and in Volvo's wind tunnel. In 1997 a second prototype, the CC, was revealed, and in 1998 the car underwent 57 different tests for international certification regulations.

The first production prototype was assembled and tested during 2000 and was premiered at that year's Paris Motor Show. In 2001, the world's press awarded the CC 8S critical acclaim and the first Koenigsegg customer took delivery in 2002.

In 2003 the CC 8S was further improved; with 655bhp and 550lb/ft of torque from its home-spun 4.7-litre (287 cubic inch) supercharged V8, it could accelerate from 0-62mph in under 3.5 seconds, cover the standing quarter-mile in 10 seconds flat with a terminal speed of 135mph and go on to a top speed in excess of 230mph.

In 2004 all development effort was concentrated on the new CCR model. Like the CC 8S, the CCR had a low-drag carbon-fiber and Kevlar body. The semi-monocoque chassis was made of carbon-fiber with honeycomb reinforcements, and suspension consisted of double wishbones at front and rear, with pushrod-operated adjustable VPS custom racing

With striking looks and alarming velocity, the CCX (left) is a true supercar, but comforts have not been sacrificed for the sake of speed (CCR interiors shown)

“ The body is made from ” carbon-fiber and Kevlar

shock absorbers and power-adjustable ride height.

The CCR's V8 featured dual Rotrex superchargers running higher boost and power was up to 806bhp at 6,900rpm with a thumping 678lb/ft of torque at 5,700rpm. Like the CC 8S, the transmission was a specially developed ultra-short-throw six-speed unit with an internal oil pump and cooler. The two-plate clutch was oil-cooled and electronically operated, and six-piston brake calipers gripped big vented discs. The wheels were Koenigsegg magnesium alloys with pressure sensors and wore 19-inch front and 20-inch rear Michelin Pilot Sport 2s.

All this gave exceptional performance. The CCR's quoted figures are: 0-62mph in 3.2 seconds, the standing quarter in 9.0 seconds at a terminal speed of 146mph and that official 241mph top speed.

Then, at the Geneva show in 2006, Koenigsegg showed off the new CCX. Though no more powerful or any faster than the CCR (their performance figures are the same), the subtly reworked CCX is designed to comply with stringent US crash test regulations. The new model is 88 millimeters (3.5 inches) longer and features increased aerodynamic downforce, optional ceramic discs and carbon-fiber wheels, improved brake cooling, better cabin ventilation, 50 millimetres (2-inches) more headroom, comfier seats and improved engine air intake flow.

Despite such massive performance, Koenigseggs are not bare-boned street racers. There is a neat detachable hardtop that stows in the front trunk, plus climate control and electrically-operated windows and mirrors. Options include parking sensors, GPS navigation, a rear-view camera, fitted luggage and a sequential gearbox.

Along with incredible speed, each Koenigsegg model has another common feature. Back in the '90s, company founder Christian von Koenigsegg decided he wanted a special door-hinge mechanism. Having approached several specialist designers who said what he required was impossible, he set about designing it himself. The result of his efforts made it to production and these masterpiece hinges use two parallel arms that rotate on a geared pivot, allowing the doors to open in a graceful outward arc. It works beautifully, and that says as much about the integrity of car as its record-breaking speed. ✺

SPECIFICATION	
ENGINE TYPE	V8 supercharged
DISPLACEMENT	4,700cc (287 cu in)
POWER	806bhp @ 6,900rpm
TORQUE	678lb/ft @ 5,700rpm
TRANSMISSION	Six-speed manual
0-62mph	3.2 seconds
TOP SPEED	245mph-plus
PRICE	€458,000 ($540,000 or (£314,000 approx) from factory, plus local taxes
www.koenigsegg.com	

The CCX (left and below) is the first model from Koenigsegg that is certified to be used on American highways, having passed US crash test regulations

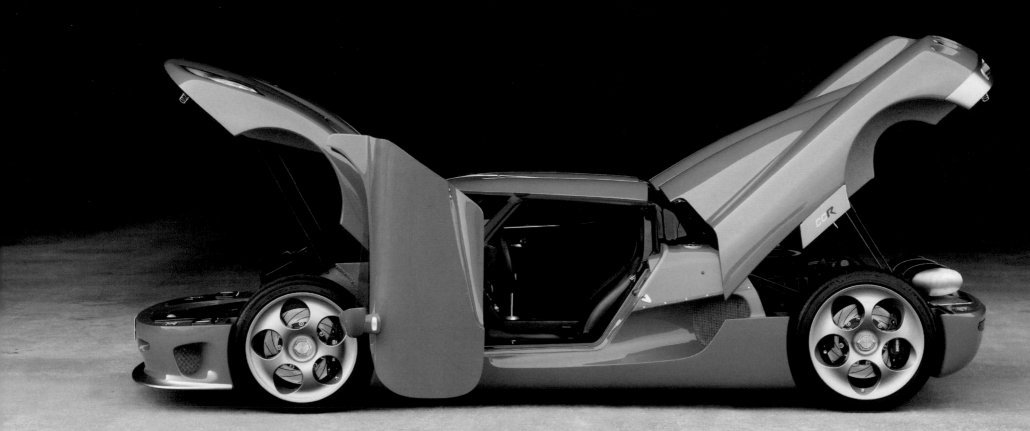

"The masterpiece hinges allow the doors to open in a graceful outward arc"

" The MC12 trounced all-comers in the world's premier race series for production-based supercars "

This Maserati may be based on Ferrari's Enzo supercar, but it's the MC12 which took the silverware in the 2005 FIA GT Championship

62

Maserati
MC12

Only the most focused supercars manage to translate huge performance and outrageous looks into race-track success. This car did just that, restoring Maserati's racing pedigree

*T*he startling MC12 came as something of a surprise when it was first revealed in 2004. For many years Maserati had been the struggling Italian underdog of the sports car world, and Fiat had saved the firm from collapse by buying it out in the early 1990s.

It was only when Fiat handed over control of the company to Ferrari later in that same decade that Maserati started to really feel the benefit. Even then, it was the Prancing Horse of Ferrari that continued to steal the limelight with a succession of increasingly superb supercars and a string of racing successes in the Formula One World Championship.

Then Maserati produced a supercar to potentially outshine even Ferrari's fabulous Enzo. Although most of the initial production run of 30 were built as road cars with just five built as racers, the real aim of the MC12 was to put Maserati back on the map in international competition, 37 long years after its last victory with a Cooper-Maserati in the 1967 South African GP.

Although the MC12 uses the Enzo's carbon-fiber and aluminum chassis, as well as its 5,998cc (366 cubic inch) V12 engine with its sequential, six-speed paddle-shift transmission, there are a number of major differences between the two cars. The most obvious is the MC12's gorgeous winged, long-tailed body that is 441mm (17.4") longer than the Ferari's. While the front and rear track measurements are

the same for both cars, the MC12's wheelbase is 150 millimeters (6 inches) longer than the Enzo's.

Although the engine size and specifications are essentially the same, Maserati claims 624bhp for the MC12 (36bhp less than Ferrari quotes for its Enzo) with top speed and 0-62mph acceleration at 'more than 205mph' and 3.8 seconds respectively. The MC12's small power deficit is no doubt down to Ferrari wishing to maintain its reputation as numero uno among sports cars and, if MC12 owners feel short changed, full Enzo power should not be too difficult to achieve with some pretty straightforward engine management adjustments.

This Maserati is certainly not the poor relation on the race track. It was the MC12 that trounced all-comers in the FIA GT championship in 2005, the world's premier race series for production-based supercars, which featured teams fielding Ferraris, Corvettes, Saleens, Aston Martins and more. This just goes to show that you can compare facts and figures all day long, but success in real competition is what speaks loudest.

With this success on the track, Maserati built a further batch of 25 MC12s in 2005, making a grand total of around 65 cars built. Compare that with a grand total of 499 Enzos and the Maserati assumes an altogether more exclusive appeal. As before, the MC12 features an all carbon-fiber body, with the front end graced by a trademark Maserati air intake featuring the company's traditional Trident logo set within. Moving to the center of the car, there's a removable hard top and just behind that an engine air intake snorkel, while at the rear a huge carbon-fiber wing, a spoiler and two pairs of elliptical exhaust tailpipes grab the attention.

Almost all the road-going MC12s have been treated to the two-tone blue and white paintjob reminiscent of the colors of the American Casner Motor Racing team which ran the famous Maserati Tipo 60-61 Birdcage racers in the early '60s.

Although basically a racer for the road, the MC12 does offer a few creature comforts such as perforated leather trim, air-conditioning, electric windows, the now traditional Maserati oval analogue clock and even a handy 12-volt power socket.

Maserati's history is steeped in racing success. Since its foundation in 1914 by Alfieri, Ettore and Ernesto Maserati, the company's cars have won 23

single-seater and sports prototype championships and 32 Formula One grand prix, including world titles in 1954 and 1957 with the legendary Juan Manuel Fangio at the wheel of the magnificent 250F. Other great drivers including Tazio Nuvolari also drove for Maserati over the years.

The company's biggest successes in sports car racing must be its Targa Florio, Buenos Aires 1000km and Nürburgring victories, while Wilbur Shaw's two wins at Indianapolis in 1939 and 1940 at the wheel of the 8CTF nicknamed the 'Boyle Special' also hold special significance, as they were the only times an Italian marque ever won the classic 500 miler.

There are supercars that are more expensive, and some with even more power and speed, but one thing's for sure. When the history books are written about the cars which managed to bring home the silverware in top-flight international competition, the Maserati MC12 will feature more strongly than most.

SPECIFICATION	
ENGINE TYPE	V12
DISPLACEMENT	5,998cc (366 cu in)
POWER	624bhp @ 7,500rpm
TORQUE	481lb/ft @ 5,500rpm
TRANSMISSION	Six-speed 'Cambiocorsa' sequential manual
0-62mph	3.8 seconds
TOP SPEED	205mph-plus
PRICE	€600,000 (£550,000 or $960,000 approx) plus local taxes
www.maserati.com	

The MC12's traditionally-shaped air intake gives the car's front end major impact, especially with Maserati's trident badge prominently displayed in the middle

Pagani
Zonda F

The result of one man's dream to build his own supercar, the Zonda is a true testament to engineering brilliance and extravagant flair. It is one of the world's wildest-looking cars

To be considered an 'ultimate', a car should excel in at least one of these areas: performance, prestige, pure road presence, technological excellence or sheer expense. The Pagani Zonda F scores high in all these categories and more, but there are few other supercars which are quite so searingly beautiful both inside and out.

After many years of dreaming, Argentinian Horacio Pagani decided to produce his own supercar in 1988. With encouragement and moral support from his fellow countryman and five-times Grand Prix World Champion Juan Manuel Fangio, Pagani set about achieving his dream. Using his considerable influence with Mercedes, Fangio proved to be instrumental in persuading the German company to supply Pagani with V12 Mercedes-Benz power for his project.

Drawing inspiration for the basic shape of the car from the Mercedes-powered Sauber Racing 'Group C' Le Mans endurance racers of the day, 25,000 hours were spent conceiving the concept, style and every engineering aspect of the new car. In 1992 Pagani founded his business in Modena, an area that had long been the heart of Italian supercar production, and built a prototype that was tested in the wind tunnel in the following year.

Following several more years of intense hard work, Pagani obtained European type approval for road use and the first Zonda C12 was revealed at the Geneva Motor Show in 1999. Named after a wind which blows through the Andes mountains of

Argentina, the Zonda stood out as something very special, even among the superstars of the supercar world. As Pagani himself explained at the time: "The Zonda's styling is supposed to make an impact, like the first time you see a really beautiful woman—she makes you go 'Wow!'"

But the car had real substance, too. The Zonda chassis consists of a carbon-fiber 'tub', with chrome-moly tubular space frames supporting the double-wishbone suspension at each end. The original C12's mid-mounted Mercedes V12 of 5,987cc (365 cubic inch) capacity produced 420bhp and 420lb/ft of torque and drove via a five-speed transmission. At 1,250kg (2,756lb), the car had an impressive power-to-weight ratio of 336bhp per tonne, and could hit 60mph in 4.5 seconds with a top speed approaching 200mph, all for the sum of 480 million Italian lire.

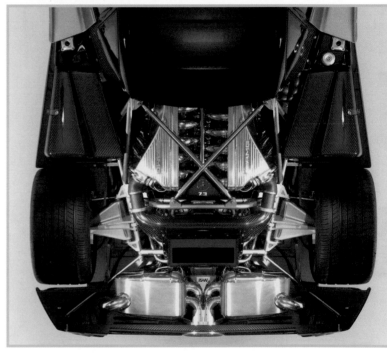

Then in 2002, as if to give its close neighbors Ferrari and Lamborghini even more to think about, Pagani launched the Zonda C12S. With aerodynamic and styling adjustments, plus a 7,291cc (455 cubic inch) V12 making 555bhp at 5,900rpm and 553lb/ft of torque at 4,050rpm, the six-speed S possessed an even better power-to-weight ratio of 444bhp per tonne. Performance was improved, with 0-60mph in 4.0 seconds and a top speed closer to 210mph. The

With its finely-crafted interior (top), a V12 giving supercar performance (center) and bodywork producing huge downforce (right), the Zonda is a superb package

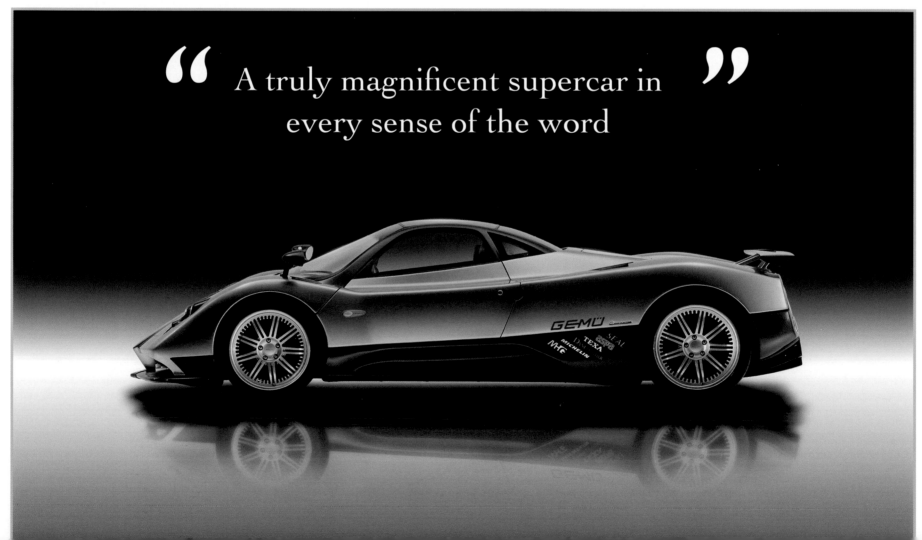

" A truly magnificent supercar in
every sense of the word "

price increased along with the performance, rising from around £195,000 ($290,000 approx.) to around £300,000 ($450,000 approx.) in the UK.

But the Zonda story doesn't end there. Sure as night follows day, along came an even more powerful, even faster Zonda F. The F's engine may be no bigger than in the S, but the higher-revving motor definitely packs a bigger punch. Power is up to 602bhp, torque to 560lb/ft, and with the optional carbon ceramic brakes fitted, the F weighs in 30kg (66lb) lighter than both the C12 and C12S. This translates to a whopping 489bhp per tonne, a 3.6 seconds 0-60mph sprint, 0-124mph in 9.8secs and a 214mph-plus top speed.

Really serious customers can opt for the F Club Sport engine which delivers 650bhp and 575lb/ft of torque equating to 528bhp per tonne, a figure which puts it on a par with the mighty Bugatti Veyron.

So, we have established that the fabulous Zonda F has bountiful beauty as well as brawn, but it steers and stops exceptionally well, too. The car's weight distribution, with 46 per cent up front and 54 per cent at the back, gives excellent balance and helps the car handle superbly. Thanks to massive 19-inch fronts and 20-inch rear Michelin Pilot Sport tires, plus 600kg (1,323lb) of aerodynamic downforce at 186mph, the Zonda F can rack up 1.4 lateral *g* in a corner, the highest claimed for any street-legal road car. Its big Brembo brakes are well up to the job—the Zonda F can brake from 124mph to a dead halt in an incredible 4.4 seconds.

It may be that Pagani, in common with the likes of Koenigsegg, Saleen and a few other newcomers, lacks the brand image of old school marques like Aston Martin, Ferrari and Lamborghini. But there's no denying that the Zonda F is beautifully engineered, superbly styled and a truly magnificent supercar in every sense of the word.

SPECIFICATION	
ENGINE TYPE	V12
DISPLACEMENT	7,291cc (445 cu in)
POWER	650bhp @ 6,200rpm (CS version)
TORQUE	575lb/ft @ 4,000rpm (CS version)
TRANSMISSION	Six-speed manual
0-62mph	3.6 seconds
TOP SPEED	214mph-plus
PRICE	£380,000 ($663,000 approx)
www.paganiautomobili.it	

The Zonda is a truly unique-looking road car. Its 'Gatling gun' exhaust pipes distinguish the rear (top left); ornate fittings and exquisite leather grace the interior (below)

Sedans

Called 'saloon' in the UK, a car with an enclosed four-door body with seating for four or more. Generally of 'three box' design comprising separate engine, passenger and luggage compartments.

Bentley Arnage

Brabus Rocket

Brabus Maybach

Rolls-Royce Phantom

"Few other production cars can be built more precisely to a customer's exact specification"

Bentley Arnage

Bentley has long been a byword for engineering excellence and luxury combined with effortless speed and good taste. The Arnage is the ultimate expression of these lofty values

Rolls-Royce and Bentley are the marques which stand out as being ultimate symbols of the best of British car craftsmanship. For 71 years both brands were under the same ownership, and for 56 of those years (until 2002) both were manufactured under the very same roof at Crewe, England. Which you prefer depends on personal preference, but of the current Crewe-built Bentleys it is the big, burly Arnage that is most representative of traditional, luxury coachbuilding.

Every Arnage is built to order and over 50% are further modified by the company's specialist Bentley Mulliner operation. Backed up by many decades of experience in building sporting limousines, few other production cars can be built more precisely to a customer's exact specification. According to one owner, determining the specification of an Arnage is like "having your own private car company", while another commented that he considered his Arnages to have been "born, not made".

With roots that can be traced back to the 1980 Mulsanne and the Mulsanne Turbo of two years later, the Arnage is a product of evolution rather than revolution. Back in 1982, a 6,750cc (412 cubic inch) Mulsanne Turbo punched out almost 300bhp, was limited to a 135mph top speed and cost £58,613 (in the region of $102,400).

Today there are three Arnage models: the R, T

and RL. All are powered by the same 6,752cc (412 cubic inch) V8, although the R and long wheelbase RL produce 400bhp and 616lb/ft of torque while the sportier T makes an extra 50bhp with a colossal 645lb/ft. Although these are big, heavy cars—the RL's wheelbase measures 3,366mm (11ft) and weighs nearly three tons—they can charge to 60mph in six seconds dead and reach 155mph. The more powerful T shaves half a second from that 0-60 time and gallops on to a heady 168mph. Think about that, almost 170mph from a 2.5-ton super-luxury sedan. It's an impressive performance. But there's more to these Bentleys than sheer speed.

The Arnage interior is as cosseting, elegant and downright luxurious as any other you could care to find. The timber used in Arnage interiors gives an insight into how this quality is achieved and the workmanship that goes into it. It takes sixteen 0.6mm (1/4") thick strips of veneer to make the 26 main veneered components, plus a further eight for the door cappings. It takes 12 to 14 days to prepare the timber, and the veneers are given five coats of lacquer and three days of curing before being wax polished by hand. Burr walnut is the most popular

Hundreds of hours of labor by master craftsmen go into the building of an Arnage, from the sumptuous interior to the glorious V8 engine and the impressive coachwork

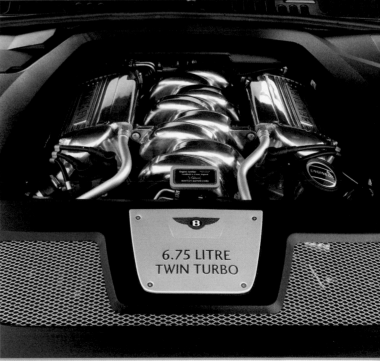

choice of veneer but, if you wish, you may use wood from your own forest.

Arnage customers also have a choice of forty exterior colors, along with seven recommended duo-tone schemes, plus 27 different hide options for the upholstery. These are all standard offerings; as a further service, under the Bentley Mulliner personalization program you can have your Arnage painted in any color of the spectrum you like, and have hides and veneers matched to your individual requirements. The only constraints in this case are imagination and taste.

If you seek exclusivity but all this choice seems too baffling, you can always opt for an Arnage 'special edition'. For example, of the 700 or so Arnages built in 2005, just 30 were 'Blue Trains', produced to celebrate the 75th anniversary of the Blue Train Race in which adventurer and three-time Le Mans 24hr winner Woolf Barnato raced his 1930 Bentley Speed Six coupe to beat the famous Blue Train express on its route across France. The 2005 Arnage Blue Train has the 450bhp engine from the Arnage T, but is distinguished by 19-inch seven-spoke alloy wheels, a chromed radiator shell and mirrors, plus stainless mesh in the front cooling ducts and quad exhaust tailpipes.

The Blue Train's interior is equally distinctive. All instrument and dial faces are black, and the centre console features a subtle Bentley Blue Train badge. The Mulliner veneers feature chrome inlays with winged 'B' badges, and the headrests have 'Blue Train' embroidered in a contrasting thread color. Other special features are its wood and leather steering wheel, additional wood panels on the doors and contrasting piping on the seats.

The Arnage is the pinnacle of engineering, luxury and customer choice. This Bentley is a real driver's car, too. It's a tough act to match, let alone beat. ※

SPECIFICATION	
ENGINE TYPE	V8 turbocharged
DISPLACEMENT	6,752cc (412 cu in)
POWER	450bhp @ 4,100rpm
TORQUE	645lb/ft @ 3,250rpm
TRANSMISSION	Four-speed auto
0-60mph	5.5 seconds
TOP SPEED	168mph
PRICE	£170,000 ($233,990) Arnage RL: £180,000 ($242,990)
www.bentleymotors.com	

Bentley customers can choose from a mindblowing range of interior and exterior appointments. A Blue Train special edition (see following pages) is a very tempting alternative

Brabus
Rocket

Compared to the other vehicles in this section, the Rocket may seem a little outclassed. But a look at its performance figures confirms that this is a real wolf in sheep's clothing

Four-door sedans don't come any faster than the astounding Brabus Rocket. With quoted performance figures of zero to 62mph in 4 seconds dead, 0-124mph in 10.5 seconds and an electronically-limited 217.5mph top speed, that is really no big surprise.

There are two-seater GTs and supercars in this book that can't match those figures, and there are those with less power, too. The Rocket's Brabus S V12 S Biturbo engine stumps up a scarcely believable 730 brake horsepower and an electronically-limited 811lb/ft of torque at just 2,100rpm. With the limiter disabled, that torque figure rises to 973lb/ft, which is more than either the SSC Ultimate Aero or Bugatti Veyron can muster. So, in case you were wondering what a Mercedes-Benz CLS with black wheels was doing within these pages, now you know.

Brabus is well known for selling custom parts and hop-up kits, but it is also an officially-registered auto manufacturer. It builds complete cars which usually start life as a stock Mercedes-Benz, but they are so heavily modified and thoroughly re-engineered that they end up as a Brabus.

Introduced in 2005, the Rocket is powered by a twin-turbo V12 from the Mercedes SL600. Brabus then drops in a special crankshaft, increases cylinder bores, fits forged pistons and installs sport camshafts. The engine is also fitted with larger turbochargers, more efficient intercoolers, free-flowing catalytic

How do you tell a Rocket from the Mercedes CLS it's based on? The quad tailpipes, bigger front air intakes and black wheels give a hint of the Brabus's tuned-up status

" The Rocket is powered by a twin-turbo **"**
V12 from the Mercedes SL600 with a
scarcely believable 730 horsepower

converters and quad tailpipes. To keep everything working in perfect harmony, the engine management system is then re-programmed.

But that's just the start. The Rocket also has a modified five-speed automatic transmission and a Brabus rear differential, plus two special suspension systems: an air-suspended, ride-levelling Comfort version, or a fully-adjustable Sport set-up with coil springs over gas shocks at both ends.

Huge vented ceramic discs with 12-piston calipers are fitted to the front, with steel discs and 6-piston calipers at the rear. Brabus fits its own multi-piece 19-inch wheels shod with either Pirelli or Yokohama tires. A special front apron with large air inlets is also fitted and the front and rear spoilers, along with other aerodynamic aids, have all been wind tunnel tested to reduce both lift and drag.

The Rocket also features Brabus's integrated entrance lights in the door sills and around the rear apron. Pushing a button on the keyless-entry remote control or pulling on a door handle activates five LED lights that light up the ground behind and on either side of the car. The stock Mercedes CLS interior is trimmed with Brabus's own leather and Alcantara, and to finish off there's a sport steering wheel and a speedo that reads to 360km/h (224mph).

The highest speed ever officially achieved by a production sedan currently stands at 217.6mph. This record was established back in the mid-'90s by a Brabus E-Class with a 6.7-liter (408 cubic inch) 640bhp V12 biturbo engine. There are few who would doubt that the more powerful, more aerodynamic Rocket has the potential go even faster, but its quoted 217.5mph maximum is electronically limited for tire safety reasons.

Of course, big fast Mercs are nothing new. Back in 1968 Mercedes launched the 300SEL 6.3. With the body of the 300SEL 3.5 and the 6.3-liter (386 cubic inch) 250bhp V8 squeezed in from the 600 limousine, it could burn up the drag strip from zero to 60mph in 6.6 seconds and hit 137mph. Aside from the Jaguar XJ12 and Maserati Quattroporte, it left all other sedans for dead.

In 1975 along came the next Mercedes supersedan, the 450SEL 6.9. The formula was basically the same, but its even bigger V8 made 286bhp and could propel the car to 60mph in 7.3 seconds, with a top speed of 144mph. Another notable muscular Merc was the 500E of the early 1990s. With a 5-liter (303 cubic inch) 322bhp V8 it could dash to 60mph in six seconds and reach 155mph.

But that was then and now is now, and what we have here in the Brabus Rocket is something which, 20 years ago, no-one would have believed possible. In the mid-'80s, even the very fastest, most exotic Italian two-seater supercars could barely manage 180mph. Today we have a five-seater luxury supersedan which sails to almost 220mph.

Isn't progress a wonderful thing. ✦

SPECIFICATION	
ENGINE TYPE	V12 turbocharged
DISPLACEMENT	6,233cc (380 cu in)
POWER	730bhp @ 5,100rpm
TORQUE	811lb/ft (limited) @ 2,100rpm (973lb/ft de-limited)
TRANSMISSION	Six-speed manual
0-62mph	4.0 seconds
TOP SPEED	217.5mph (electronically limited)
PRICE	€391,000 (£267,600, $465,500 approx) + tax
www.brabus.com	

Aerodynamic aids, including the front and rear spoilers, have been tested in a wind tunnel to reduce lift and drag

"This is an elite, super-luxury limo"

Brabus Maybach

More than just a car, this is more like a private jet for the road.

Only the biggest high-rollers have the means for a Maybach

Luxury limousines are a common sight in big cities. But the Maybach 57 and longer-wheelbase 62 models represent the elite, super-luxury limos only inhabited by the wealthiest businessmen and the biggest stars.

The first modern, Mercedes-developed Maybach arrived on the scene in New York in July 2002, having been shipped from Europe on the luxury QE2 passenger liner. Unlike ordinary limos, which are little more than stretched sedans, the Maybach was designed as a super-limousine from scratch and, once inside, the difference is blindingly obvious. And then there's the hyper-limo Brabus Maybach...

The basic, longer-wheelbase Maybach 62 costs $385,250 (£298,900 in the UK) and is over 20ft long, so there's plenty of room to stretch out on the powered rear seats with extending leg and footrests and recline to almost horizontal. In the unlikely event that there's nobody at hand to close your door, all you have to do is touch a nearby button and the door will close itself. Then you may wish to

The Maybach's rear seats can recline to near horizontal, and even feature an air-activated massaging function

smoke a cigar from the car's humidor or sip vintage champagne chilled in the car's champagne cooler. And while you're relaxing you can choose from the seat's heating or cooling functions, or enjoy the air-activated massage function, and perhaps adjust the interior lighting via the liquid-crystal panorama roof while you watch a DVD movie played thru a 12 amp, 21-speaker, 600-watt surround sound system.

With a choice of six leather colors, three types of fine wood and 17 exterior paint finishes (which can be combined for a two-tone scheme), Maybach customers have over two million permutations of standard and optional equipment to choose from.

Maybach engineers also ensured there was enough power up front to haul the 62's 3,380 kilos (7,452lbs) around at a very respectable pace. Its twin-turbo, 5,513cc (336 cubic inch) V12 pumps out 550bhp and 663lb/ft of torque, enabling the big 62 to sprint from zero to 62mph in 5.4 seconds (5.2 secs for the slightly lighter 57) and reach 155mph.

For those seeking even sportier performance, Maybach has introduced the 57 S. Powered by a 604bhp AMG-tuned V12, the six-liter (366 cubic inch) S version charges from 0 to 60mph in under five seconds and hits 172mph. Twenty-inch 11-spoke wheels, lower-profile tires and a lowered chassis with stiffened suspension give sportier handling without sacrificing the car's ride comfort too much.

At this point you'd think common sense would prevail and that anyone wanting more than a 172mph super-limo would need their head examining. But that hasn't stopped the boys at Brabus (for whom no Mercedes, McLaren Mercedes or Maybach is too sacred) from taking things a step further.

For the ultimate ultra-limo, Brabus engineers developed a special longer-stroke crankshaft as well as special con-rods and upped capacity to 6.3 liters (384 cu in) with bigger bores and pistons. This SV12 Biturbo engine conversion also includes re-worked cylinder heads, custom camshafts, revised engine management mapping and a re-designed exhaust system with two ultra-slim tailpipes.

Performance is increased from the implausible to the unbelievable; the Brabus Maybach 57 version accelerates from 0-62 in 4.9 seconds and has a max of 195mph. To cope with such speed, the Brabus runs on 21-inch wheels, with the air-suspension ride height lowered by 15 millimeters (3/5 inches). The

Brabus also has two auxiliary headlights and LED lights illuminating the ground around the car.

Stepping inside, you'll find Brabus's own leather trim and sheepskin floormats, as well as 15-inch flatscreens (up from 9-inch) and a computer custom-developed for use in a car with an 80GB hard drive. This is connected to the internet (via UMTS) and has a wireless keyboard with optical mouse. There is even a USB port in the rear center console for peripherals such as a digital camera.

To remain online even after leaving the car, there's an IBM X Series notebook in an electrically-operated drawer in the trunk. This is connected with the car's PC network via W-LAN. An additional 6-disc DVD changer completes the interior.

Of course, this amazing Brabus could conceivably be gold-plated and have diamond-studded wheels, but then it might not make it to these pages on the grounds of good taste. ▧

SPECIFICATION	
ENGINE TYPE	V12 turbocharged
DISPLACEMENT	6,300cc (384 cu in)
POWER	640bhp @ 5,100rpm
TORQUE	757lb/ft @ 1,750rpm
TRANSMISSION	Five-speed auto
0-62mph	4.9 seconds (57)
TOP SPEED	195mph (57)
PRICE	62: €528,319 (approx £362,000 or $629,000) plus local taxes
www.brabus.com	

A high-powered limousine for powerful people, the Brabus Maybach also provides a high-tech work environment for the time-pressed business mogul

Rolls-Royce
Phantom

If you really want to impress people, you have to arrive in a Phantom. It says you're something special, whether you are a chart-topping rapper or a member of a royal family

Bugatti, Cadillac, Duesenberg, Maybach and Mercedes-Benz have all, at one time or another, laid claim to being the maker of the world's most prestigious luxury automobiles. But over the past century it is Rolls-Royce which has been the most consistent. The current Phantom may not be the longest, most powerful or even the most expensive super-luxury sedan, but this magnificent car exudes breeding, status and an assertive presence that no other can match.

Rolls-Royce's first Phantom model went on sale in 1925. A replacement for the Silver Ghost, the 85mph Phantom I had a 108bhp, 7,668cc (468 cubic inch) straight six-cylinder engine and was built at Derby in the UK and in Springfield, USA. This was followed in 1929 by the 92mph Phantom II, which used the same basic engine but had a greatly improved chassis.

The Phantom III was launched in 1936, powered by the first Rolls-Royce V12 motor. With a capacity of 7,340cc (448 cubic inches) it could accelerate to 60mph in less than 17 seconds, even with heavy coachwork. The Phantom IV appeared in 1950 and, at over 19 feet in length and with a 5,677cc (346 cubic inch) straight-eight, just 18 were built for royalty and heads of state. The Phantom V and VI models were manufactured between 1959 and 1991 and used the Silver Cloud's V8 engine on a stretched, steel-framed Cloud chassis.

But the story of the current Phantom started in 1998 when, after 94 years of British ownership,

BMW bought the famed marque. The German company's 322bhp, 5.4-liter (329 cubic inch) V12 engine soon migrated from the 7-Series to the new Silver Seraph and, with assistance from BMW, this was the first all-new Rolls-Royce in 32 years.

At the same time, work on 'Project Rolls-Royce' began in earnest. The London-based design team first identified the most significant models from the

The Phantom is a cut above regular run-of-the-mill super-sedans. The quality and breeding stand out a mile

past. For example, the Phantom II incorporated many of the important Rolls-Royce design elements, including large wheels and a long bonnet. The 1960s Silver Shadow had a modern, straightforward appearance, but the designers judged the '50s Silver Cloud as representing the essence of post-war Rolls-Royce style. All three models personify the air of authority expected from a Rolls-Royce, and this is expertly captured in today's Phantom.

Phantom occupants enjoy elevated seating which places them above most other road users. The driver's eye-line is midway between that of a conventional sedan and a large SUV, while rear passengers sit 18 millimeters (3/4") higher than those in the front. Rear passengers also have the benefit of rear-hinged coach doors which not only contain umbrellas, but also allow far easier and more elegant access. They also 'soft close' at the touch of a button. The interior of the Phantom is appointed with sheepskin rugs, a 600-watt surround-sound audio system and even an optional, individual theatre system.

Although this Rolls-Royce is technologically very advanced, traditional features abound, such as the organ-stop and violin-key-shaped switches. And while a tachometer has long been considered unnecessary in a Rolls-Royce, today's Phantom has a power reserve gauge which shows, for example, that as it whispers along at 100mph the engine has 75% of its total power capability left.

Up to 16 hides are used to trim each Phantom and the leather used is the softest in the industry. All 450 leather pieces in the car are cut using a laser guide, but hand-finishing ensures that top quality is achieved. Six different veneers are available for the 60 separate wood pieces, and every surface, be it wood, leather or wool, is the genuine article. For the exterior, there are 68 basic color themes to choose from, plus 15 different interior colors—and that's without considering hand-painted coachlines or Rolls-Royce's custom Bespoke program.

Naturally, power and performance from the 6.75-liter (412 cu in) V12 is 'ample', to use a typically understated English word. With a very high-tech aluminum space-frame chassis, perfect 50/50 front/rear weight distribution, automatically-controlled air suspension and ultra-sophisticated Michelin PAX run flat tires, comfort and safety are assured along with precision handling.

There is one final touch: the Phantom's enormous 31-inch diameter wheels feature synchronized centers to ensure that the interlinked 'RR' badges on all four wheels always remain in an upright position. As Sir Henry Royce once said: "Accept nothing nearly right, or good enough". ✶

SPECIFICATION	
ENGINE TYPE	V12
DISPLACEMENT	6,749cc (412 cu in)
POWER	453bhp @ 5,350rpm
TORQUE	531lb/ft @ 3,500rpm
TRANSMISSION	Six-speed auto
0-60mph	5.7 seconds
TOP SPEED	149mph (limited)
PRICE	£250,000 ($328,750)
www.rolls-roycemotorcars.com	

Supreme elegance is the hallmark of the Phantom, both in the sumptuous interior and the impressive coachwork

" The Phantom personifies the air of authority that you expect from a Rolls-Royce "

SUVs

Acronym for Sport Utility Vehicle. A car with on and off-road capabilities, due in part to increased ground clearance and all-wheel drive. Features 'two box' body style with tailgate and seating for five or more.

Hummer H1 Alpha

International 7300 CXT

Kombat T-98

Overfinch Range Rover SuperSport

Porsche Cayenne Turbo S

& Sportec SP600M

"The H1 Alpha represents the single greatest advance in the 14-year history of the civilian Hummer"

Hummer
H1 Alpha

The H1 Alpha still has the unmistakable looks of the first Hummer. But, as you'll discover, this is much, much more than merely a military vehicle with civilian license plates

Amidst all the smart bombs, daisy cutters, Tomahawk cruise missiles, Thunderbolts, B2 Stealth bombers, F-16s and other hardware used by American forces during the 1991 Gulf War, there was one, simpler military machine which more than any other captured the imagination of the billions of TV viewers watching the Desert Storm saga unfold—the Humvee.

Like the Willys Jeep (now called the Wrangler) that saw active service in previous conflicts, the Humvee was also destined to become a desirable cult vehicle on Civilian Street. But the progression from a funky-looking military vehicle to the 2006 Hummer H1 Alpha on sale in showrooms today didn't happen overnight.

Back in 1979, AM General (formerly American Motors) started designing a High Mobility Multi-Purpose Wheeled Vehicle (HMMWV) to meet US Army standards. The two other companies also competing for this lucrative contract were Teledyne and Chrysler Defense, and they both already had advanced designs on their drawing boards. Although AM General appeared to be well behind the others, the company had no preconceived design notions, so it simply rolled up its sleeves and created an original design classic from scratch.

Those army specifications were very stringent, with demands for light armor, deep-water fording

capability as well as Arctic and desert operational ability, to name but a few. On top of that, there had to be absolute reliability, durability and maintainability. Vehicle weight constraints also called for breakthroughs in material development. All of this and AM General had a deadline of just ten months to

The Hummer's incredible all-terrain ability makes it a big military success. The H1 Alpha translates that ability to civilian life, with added power and creature comforts

More like a command centre than a vehicle interior, the Hummer's cabin (left) gives a supreme sense of dominating the road

complete it—quite a challenge for any vehicle maker.

Over the next few years, AM General built a number of prototypes which were rigorously tested and evaluated, and the company was subsequently awarded an initial contract for 55,000 vehicles, with volume Humvee production starting in 1985. In 1989 a further 33,331 military Humvees were ordered, and the following year—one year prior to the Gulf War—initial design work for a civilian Hummer was set in motion.

Four months after cessation of hostilities in the Gulf, AM General announced its intent to make a civilian Hummer for sale to the general public. Though neither foreseen nor intentional, the Humvee's prominent role in the war meant that no motor manufacturer ever had a promotional campaign quite like it.

In 1992 volume production began and, at the same time as the 100,000th military Humvee was produced, the first civilian Hummer was delivered. Save for a few refinements, this was essentially unchanged from its military counterpart, with the same basic design and components.

In 1996 the first turbodiesel Hummer was launched at the Detroit Auto Show, and in late 1999 AM General sold the Hummer name along with the marketing and distribution rights to General Motors, but continued to manufacture the original Hummer H1.

Seven years later, the H1 Alpha model hit the streets. Representing the single greatest advance in the 14-year history of the civilian vehicle, the Alpha delivers an 18% improvement in torque (520lb/ft), 0-60mph acceleration in 13.5 seconds and a greater towing capacity than the previous model—its Gross Combined Weight Rating is now 17,300lb (7,847 kg). The H1 Alpha also enjoys 46% more horsepower from its 300bhp, 403 cubic inch (6,599cc) V8 Duramax engine, enhanced off-road crawling and climbing capability plus an improved fuel range of almost 600 miles.

It is the wheels' geared hubs that contribute to this truck's incredible crawling and climbing ability, and they have been redesigned to feature a helical-cut gear set. To accommodate the new engine and transmission, the H1 Alpha's body is positioned two inches higher than the previous H1's, giving even more minimum ground clearance, now at 16 inches

(406mm). The brakes have also been improved.

Although the Hummer has always been more about performance than style, there are a few visual enhancements. The 17-inch wheels now have a brighter finish, but retain the run-flat capability and CTIS (Central Tire Inflation System) with on-board air compressor and concealed air delivery system, and the interior features leather seats and more luxurious surfaces.

What really qualifies the near seven-foot-wide Hummer for inclusion on these pages is that it can do things no other vehicle can do. It can scale 22-inch (559mm) rock ledges, ford 30 inches (762 mm) of water and climb 60% grades.

These uncompromised, unrivalled off-roading capabilities enable the battle-hardened H1 to stake a genuine claim to the title of the ultimate all-terrain vehicle in the world today.

SPECIFICATION	
ENGINE TYPE	V8 diesel
DISPLACEMENT	403 cu in (6,599cc)
POWER	300bhp @ 3,000rpm
TORQUE	520lb/ft @ 1,500rpm
TRANSMISSION	Five-speed auto, 4WD
0-60mph	13.5 seconds
TOP SPEED	90mph (approx)
PRICE	Closed Wagon: $139,771 (approx £79,600)
www.hummer.com	

The H1 Alpha's 403 cubic inch V8 Duramax engine produces nearly 50% more power than the old unit

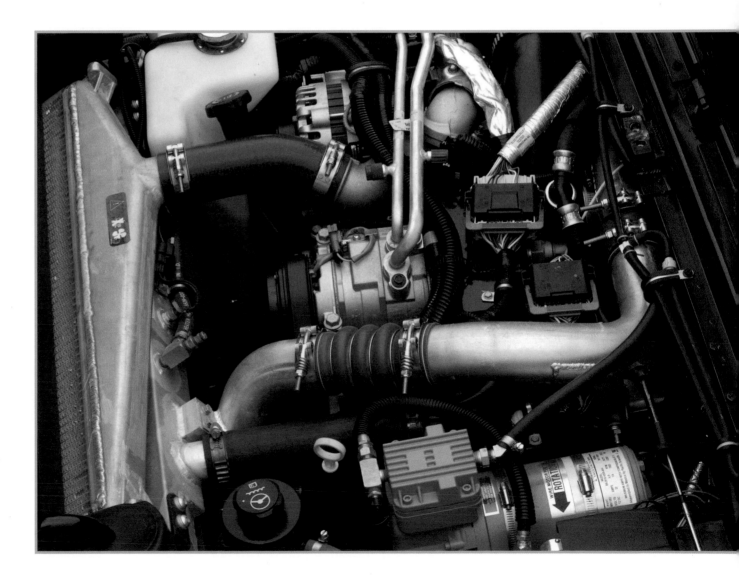

International
CXT 7300

If you need living proof that everything's bigger in Texas, just take a look at the CXT 7300. At first glance, it looks like a big rig, but this monster is actually a pick-up truck!

Okay, first things first; this thing is BIG. In fact, the International 7300 CXT is the world's biggest production pick-up truck, and it's so darn big you can hardly believe it. At 21 feet long, with tires hip-high and a 9-foot tall cab, it can haul 6 tons, seat a football team's offensive line and, for grown-up kids who miss playing with their trucks in the sandbox, it is the ultimate toy.

Granted, technically the all-wheel-drive CXT (short for Commercial Extreme Truck) may not be a 'car' in the strictest sense of the word, but where's the law which says that Sport Utility Vehicles have to be cars and not trucks?

The giant CXT was first unveiled in the fall of 2004 at International's manufacturing plant in Garland, Texas. At the time, Garland's proud mayor Bob Day announced: "The International CXT brings new meaning to 'everything is big in Texas'. There is nothing on the road as bold, strong and tough as this truck." Bob, you're not wrong.

Born of a 20-ton hauler truck more normally used in the construction and waste industries, the CXT is built on the same chassis as dump trucks and snow-ploughs. As a result, it really is unrivalled in capability, size and appearance. It hauls three times the payload of consumer pick-up trucks, it has huge, hissing air brakes (which were designed for 13-ton loads) and offers exceptional towing and load-lugging capability.

The CXT also features a spacious interior with an air-suspended four-door double-crew cab that seats five (with standard front air seats) and can be customized to meet owners' specific needs—from paint color to air seats to flat-screen TVs. So those with Godzilla-sized egos who really want to make a bigger statement could order a customized black CXT with ghosted green flames, a leather interior with wood grain trim, reclining captain's chairs, a fold-down bench that can be used as a bed, an overhead compartment with drop-down DVD, a satellite radio system and a rear-mounted camera for better rearward visibility when reversing.

Behind the enormous polished chrome grille there's an International DT 466 cubic inch (7.6-liter) turbocharged, 24-valve diesel engine which lazily delivers up to 220bhp with a thumping 540lb/ft of torque, so it's capable of hauling or towing pretty much anything you can put into it or hitch behind it. To be more precise, the CXT has a gross vehicle weight of 25,999lb (11,793kg) and so is rated to haul a massive 12,000lb (5,443kg) payload.

Should 220 horses not quite measure up to your requirements or expectations, International makes this engine with 10 different power outputs, so you

The air-suspended double crew cab can be customized with different paint colors, flat-screen TVs, air seats, wood grain trim and a fold-down bench that can be used as a bed

"For grown-up kids who miss playing with their trucks in the sand box, this is the ultimate toy"

Whether you're loading up Canada geese or enough boxes of groceries to last you for months, the loadbay is a bit of a stretch, with sides over six feet high

could decide to go for a 245bhp version, or a 255bhp, 260bhp, 285bhp or even a 300bhp version that punches out a seriously heavyweight 860lb/ft of torque. To keep things nice and easy from the driver's perspective, the big turbodiesel is coupled to a smooth-shifting Allison five-speed auto transmission with all-wheel-drive selectable when required. Being a commercial truck engine, the DT 466 also offers extended serviceability and long-term durability, and so is designed to run to the moon and back (or 500,000 miles) between engine overhauls.

The CXT is one BIG beast, and now it's time to tell you precisely how big: its overall length is 21.46 feet (6.54 meters), it is 8 feet (2.44 meters) wide, its cab height is 9 feet (2.75 meters), the standard flatbed length is 8 feet (2.44 meters) and it sits 4.8 feet (1.46 meters) from the ground. The top of the bed's sides are 6.42 feet (1.96 meters) high and the whole thing weighs about 14,000lb (6,350kg) unladen, give or take a few ounces.

There are some who may wonder just what the point of all this excess is, but you have to look at it this way. If you had been manufacturing commercial delivery vans and trucks for over a hundred years, as International now has, wouldn't you occasionally want to make something glamorous, too; something which really made people look twice, something ultimate? Sure you would. ▧

SPECIFICATION	
ENGINE TYPE	In-line six-cylinder turbodiesel
DISPLACEMENT	466 cu in (7,639cc)
POWER	220bhp-plus, governed @ 2,600rpm (see text)
TORQUE	540+lb/ft (see text)
TRANSMISSION	Five-speed auto, on demand 4WD
0-60mph	n/a
TOP SPEED	n/a
PRICE	$117,700 (approx. £67,000)
www.internationaldelivers.com	

With a smooth-shifting Allison five-speed transmission and selectable all-wheel drive, the CXT makes light work of most on-road or off-road situations

Kombat
T-98

In a world blighted by terrorism, it makes sense to get maximum protection. The Kombat T-98 is unsurpassed when it comes to keeping its occupants out of harm's way

Naturally you would expect to see Ferraris, Lamborghinis, Porsches and Rolls-Royces among theses pages, but probably not a Russian vehicle. So, you're probably wondering, what is a Kombat T-98 and what's it doing here?

The answers are simple. First, the company claims that the T-98 is 'the fastest armored four-wheel-drive vehicle in the world'. Second, how many cars can you think of which can come equipped with the highest B7-level ballistic protection (able to stop a 12.7mm bullet) to the sides, roof, cabin and engine bay, and have an underbody which can withstand the blast from hand grenades and anti-personnel mines?

The 'Fast Attack' and 'Special Operations' T-98s can even be equipped with a vehicle-mounted 23mm gun, plus 7.62mm, 12.7mm and 14.5mm machine guns and a remote-controlled grenade launching system. The T-98 gives the expression 'road rage' a whole new meaning.

The Saint Petersburg-based Armoring Group responsible for the T-98 first took root back in 1985. Its first two prototypes were 'Laura' sports coupes with Lada engines and 'hand-made' suspension, steering and front-wheel-drive systems. By order of the Soviet Ministry of Transport, the company then built a sleek Lada-powered minivan. Then came a small 4WD SUV, a truck cabin, another small two-seater 4x4, a second Laura (with Audi turbo power), several armored security vans based on Russian and

US vehicles, a third Laura based on the Pontiac Fiero and a series of robust, working 4x4 SUVs.

The T-98 uses a number of major US-sourced components including the 8.1-litre (494 cubic inch) petrol engine, suspension, electrics and controls from General Motors. The transmission is from Allison, as used in the H1 Hummer, with an Autotrac dual-range 4WD transfer case. The dashboard and instrument panels are from a Chevy Suburban.

Suspension is independent at the front with dual-stage multi-leaf springs at the rear, and wheels are 17-inch (20-inch optional) with BF Goodrich All Terrain tires. The brakes have ABS anti-lock and DRP (Dynamic Rear Proportioning), a system which recognizes rear brake lock-up and regulates the pressure applied at the rear.

In stock trim this 'Vortec' V8 puts out 340bhp, which is good for a 9 to 10.5 second 0-60mph time, depending on armor level (a B6 level T-98 Station Wagon weighs in at 4,150kg or 9,149lbs) and a top speed of 111mph. A torquey 'Duramax' 6.6-liter (403 cubic inch) turbodiesel, also used by the H1 Hummer, is also available, but customers requiring more power can opt for a supercharged V8 which pumps out 600bhp. This cuts the 0-60mph time to

Thinking of taking a trip to a war zone or convinced someone's out to get you? The T-98 is the answer

" According to its makers, it's
impossible to equip even a Hummer
with this level of protection "

six seconds and bumps top speed up to 124mph.

A light-armor T-98 like the one illustrated here costs €124,000 (approx £84,000 or $147,000) plus local taxes and shipping, but full B7 armor pushes the price up to around €190,000 (around £129,000 or $226,000), and the budget would have to stretch further still for the supercharged 600bhp motor...

That's a lot of money for what could loosely be described as a re-bodied GM SUV, but it is the body which is the T-98's big selling point. Made from high-quality bulletproof German steel, it is extraordinarily tough. The protective shell is double-skinned and features what's described as a 'cellular filler between a metal-ceramic sandwich'. This technology allows substantially higher protection levels than can be achieved in conventional armored passenger vehicles. According to the T-98's makers, it's impossible to equip even a Hummer with this level of protection. In addition, the T-98's very special 50mm thick glass can withstand an armor-piercing bullet.

Of course, the politicians, oligarchs and business barons who require such protection don't want to be rattled about in the inside of a stark, military-spec vehicle. They need comfort at least as much as the rest of us, so the T-98 owner basks in a level of luxury not normally enjoyed by the average combat soldier. The T-98 has a leather and wood trimmed interior, equipped with dual-zone climate control, satellite radio and 6-disc CD changer, twin airbags, cruise control, trip computer and eight-way power-adjustable seats.

On the outside, there are heavy-duty fenders, light-sensitive automatic headlamps, custom paint and a remote keyless entry system, while the options list includes custom interior design, a TV and DVD player, an auxiliary engine heater for cold climates, bi-Xenon headlamps, a front-mounted winch and a long-wheelbase chassis.

So, as SUVs go, the Kombat is pretty special, and although it's bulletproof body doesn't have the sex appeal of a curvaceous Italian supercar, the T-98 does look seriously cool. ▨

SPECIFICATION (also see text)	
ENGINE TYPE	V8 or V8 turbodiesel
DISPLACEMENT	8,100cc (494 cu in) petrol or 6,599cc (403 cu in) turbodiesel
POWER	340bhp @ 4,200rpm (petrol), 300bhp @ 3,100rpm (turbodiesel)
TORQUE	455lb/ft @ 3,200rpm (petrol), 520lb/ft @ 1,800rpm (turbodiesel)
TRANSMISSION	Dual-range five-speed auto, 4WD
0-60mph	9.0 seconds
TOP SPEED	111mph
PRICE	€124,000 (approx £84,300 or $147,250) + tax (model shown)
www.armoringgroup.com	

Well, would you mess with a Kombat T-98?

" The most exotic and the most powerful version of one of the world's greatest SUVs "

Overfinch Range Rover
SuperSport

The original Range Rover was a go-anywhere machine with enhanced luxury. Overfinch's version of its latest incarnation is a go-faster machine with added horsepower

Few cars can lay claim to being the very first of their kind, but the Range Rover is one. It was not the first SUV—Jeep's Wagoneer, for example, had been introduced seven years before the Range Rover's launch in 1970—but the Range Rover was the first luxury SUV.

The Range Rover was blessed with the comfort and on-road driving qualities to rival the finest sedans of the day, while at the same time being capable of crossing the kind of awkward terrain that was previously only attempted by skillful Land Rover and Jeep CJ drivers.

Over the decades the Range Rover has, just like other models with similar longevity, been reworked, redesigned and refined to keep it competitive. But since the mid-'80s it has been the small independent British firm Overfinch that, by re-engineering Range Rovers for enhanced on-road performance, has often led the way.

The company achieved this either by enlarging and tuning the stock Buick/Rover V8 motor, or by fitting a small-block Chevy V8 hopped-up to deliver significantly superior performance. At the same time, Overfinch would upgrade suspension and brakes, and invariably make subtle bodywork mods while also re-appointing the interior to produce a customized vehicle inside and out.

In 2005 a new Range Rover model appeared which, for a moment or two, could have taken the wind out of Overfinch's sails. Called the Range Rover Sport, it was built to compete with more road-orientated SUVs such the BMW X5. Although the new Sport model has not sacrificed any of the Range Rover's traditional and considerable off-road

Overfinch do not do things by halves. Their tuning mods to the Range Rover Sport's motor include a custom-built crankshaft: the result is a hop up from 390bhp to 515bhp

Everything about the Overfinch Supersport screams high performance. Especially in this outrageous orange colour scheme

prowess, its looks are certainly more urban than rural and it's performance is definitely more Jaguar than Land Rover. To put it another way, it was pretty much what had been putting food on the table at Overfinch all these years.

The top Range Rover Sport uses a supercharged 4.2-litre V8 derived from the engine used in Jaguar performance models, but specially developed for Land Rover needs. Power is fed, full-time, to all four wheels through a ZF six-speed 'intelligent shift' automatic gearbox.

Although the new Sport delivers exceptional SUV performance (of the kind which discerning Range Rover customers had previously gone knocking on Overfinch's door to achieve) Overfinch was not unduly perturbed. In fact, the firm was well prepared, as its new engine for the new Overfinch SuperSport had been in development by engineers since it was known which engine the top Range Rover Sport would use back in 2003.

By applying the same logic as before, they took the stock 4.2-liter V8 and bored and stoked it to 5 liters. This required a new custom-built high-strength steel crankshaft, new forged pistons, new shot-peened steel con-rods and custom-made cast iron cylinder liners. The cylinder head ports and intake ducting were also modified along with an uprated supercharger, a free-flow stainless steel sports exhaust system with quad tailpipes and a re-mapped engine control unit.

All this meant that power was bumped up from 390bhp to 515bhp, with torque up from a meaty 410lb/ft to a substantially beefier 576lb/ft, giving a marked improvement in performance. The stock Range Rover Sport can accelerate from 0-60mph in 7.2 seconds and power onto a 148mph top speed. The Overfinch SuperSport beats that by sprinting to 60mph in just 5.6 seconds, and it can bully its way right up to 160mph.

Of course, if you're going to drive that fast, you'll need heavy-duty brakes, all exclusively made for Overfinch by Brembo. And while you're at it, you may as well fit Overfinch Tiger 22-inch wheels, a 10-piece Overfinch styling pack with front spoiler, side skirts and rear undertray with built-in diffuser, as well as a full custom interior. All of this can bump the price up to the region of £115,000 (over $200,000) compared to the £60,000 (in the region

of $70,000 in the US) of the standard Range Rover Sport which Overfinch uses as the basis on which its Supersport is created.

In 1970, the all-new Range Rover went on sale in the UK for £1,998 (about $4,800). Its 3.5-liter V8 made 135bhp, while the final 4.5-liter version of 2001 made 225bhp. Even then it would have been inconceivable that just five years later there would be a Range Rover with 521bhp which handled more like a good sports car.

The Overfinch SuperSport is the most exotic, most powerful and the finest version of the one of the world's greatest SUVs, and you don't get much better than that. ▩

SPECIFICATION	
ENGINE TYPE	V8 supercharged
DISPLACEMENT	4,996cc
POWER	515bhp @ 5,750rpm
TORQUE	576lb/ft @ 3,200rpm
TRANSMISSION	Six-speed auto
0-60mph	5.6 seconds
TOP SPEED	160mph
PRICE	from £95,000 ($166,800) to £115,000 ($201,900) approx
www.overfinch.com	

Overfinch offer a full custom interior service

"With 521bhp, the Turbo S" is the second most powerful production Porsche ever

Porsche Cayenne Turbo S and Sportec SP600M

When Porsche said they were going to build an SUV, we knew it was going to be special. But these two versions of the Cayenne are more than that, they're simply outrageous

N ot so long ago, the only road cars capable of much over 160mph were exotic GTs or supercars. But times have changed. We now have a handful of 220mph-plus supercars, sedans that can top 200mph and even a couple of four-wheel-drive SUVs that can manage 160mph or more. Now meet the 167mph Porsche Cayenne Turbo S, the world's fastest standard production SUV.

It was first publicly announced in July 1997 that Porsche and Volkswagen were planning to join forces to produce an all-new SUV, with Porsche taking full responsibility for the car's design and development. (VW's version is called the Touareg.) Five years and two months on, the Cayenne was proudly presented at the 2002 Paris Motor Show.

Until recently there were three basic Cayennes: the 250bhp V6 entry model, the 340bhp V8 Cayenne S and the 450bhp twin-turbocharged V8 Cayenne Turbo. The normally aspirated Cayenne S can hit 150mph while the Turbo can do the 0-62mph dash in 5.6 seconds and reach a 165mph top speed. That is impressive enough, but even more so when you consider that despite the car's sports car handling and dizzying speed, the Cayenne is also an extremely rugged and capable off-road tool.

However, for reasons best known to Porsche, 450bhp was judged insufficient for the top-of-the-range Cayenne Turbo, so in early 2006 the company launched the Turbo S. Featuring increased turbo boost pressure, upgraded intercoolers and tweaked

engine management, the Turbo S puts out 71 horse-power more than the previous Turbo model. With 521bhp, the new model is the second most power-ful series production Porsche ever (after the 612bhp Carrera GT) and can reach 167mph. As regards acceleration, the Turbo S cuts down the 0-62mph

The Cayenne is fast, even by Porsche standards, with acceleration that ranks alongside some 911 models

The Turbo S benefits from increased performance compared to the previous models, while retaining the Cayenne's competence off-road. An Advanced Off-road upgrade is available, too

time to just 5.2 seconds. That is identical to the time Porsche quotes for the 2006-model 911 Carrera 2 Cabrio and a tenth of a second quicker than the all-wheel-drive 911 Carrera 4 Cabrio. That makes the Cayenne Turbo S a very fast vehicle indeed, even by Porsche standards.

On the road considerable care is required when hoofing the throttle. In fact, hoofing is far too strong a word, because even the gentlest caress of the pedal prompts the Turbo S into surging forward with neck-bending speed. Accompanied by the V8's aggressive growl, this storming acceleration doesn't seem to diminish until there's 150mph showing on both the digital and analogue speedometers.

Additional Turbo S upgrades include self-leveling air suspension (with Porsche Active Suspension Management) as standard, plus bigger brake discs and calipers. Apart from larger 20-inch wheels and different badging, the Turbo S also wears a subtly redesigned front air grille, along with oval rather than rectangular section tailpipes.

As mentioned, the speedy Cayenne is also a very competent off-roader. Those owners who wish to venture some a good way from the blacktop should be equipped with that air suspension, while those seeking serious adventure should go for the Advanced Off-road pack. This includes hydraulically disengage-able front and rear anti-roll bars, an electronically variable rear differential lock (in addition to the standard electronic centre diff lock) as well as sill-protecting rockrails with skid-plates, a reinforced engine bay guard and extra underside protection for the fuel tank and rear axle. Finally, if you want to reap the full benefit of all that technology, a set of Pirelli Scorpion all-terrain tyres is recommended.

However, it would appear that there's demand from some individuals who are happy to sacrifice a good amount of the Cayenne's off-road capabilities in the quest for even greater speed. The Sportec Cayenne SP600M is here to meet their needs.

Swiss tuning firm Sportec takes the standard Cayenne V8 Turbo model and makes it into something even more extraordinary. The Stage 3 engine tune includes internal engine modifications, Sportec specification turbochargers, modified fuelling and engine management systems and a high performance exhaust with a 'sports' catalytic converter.

With an almost insane 600bhp and 600lb/ft on tap, it's advisable to also opt for the full aerodynamic body kit, as well as upgrades to suspension, wheels, brakes and tires. And while you're having all that done, you may as well tick the boxes for interior adornments such as an aluminum pedal set and some carbon-fiber trim.

The net result of the full 'Sportecification' is a Cayenne that Sportec conservatively estimates will max out at 186mph. The fact of the matter is that the Sportec SP600M holds the world SUV speed record of 191.66mph. Of course, it may not be too long before we have a 200mph SUV, but for now at least, this is the ultimate.

SPECIFICATION	
ENGINE TYPE	V8 turbocharged
DISPLACEMENT	4,511cc (275 cu in)
POWER	521bhp @ 5,500rpm (Sportec 600bhp @ 6,000rpm)
TORQUE	531lb/ft @ 2,750 to 3,750rpm (Sportec 600lb/ft @ 3,000rpm)
TRANSMISSION	Six-speed Tiptronic S
0-62mph	5.2secs (Sportec 4.2secs)
TOP SPEED	167mph (Sportec 186mph/see text)
PRICE	£81,565/$111,600 (Sportec: Cayenne V8 Turbo + £37,000 $65,000 approx)
www.porsche.com or www.sportec.ch	

The Sportec SP600M is the holder of the official world speed record for an SUV, at an incredible 191.66mph

US Supercars

A two-seater car designed and/or manufactured in the USA with striking appearance, surplus horsepower and extreme dynamic performance, acceleration and top speed.

Ford GT

Hennessey Venom 1000

Mosler MT900S

Saleen S7 Twin Turbo

SSC Ultimate Aero

" A truly modern supercar that is **"**
much more civilized than its ancestor

Ford GT

The modern-day Ford GT is a reborn American icon, inspired by the world-class race car of four decades ago

Maybe more than any other car featured in these pages, this legendary automobile has heritage oozing from every mechanical pore. The Ford GT is a true 'great' with a story that stretches back to the 1960s.

Back in 1963, Henry Ford II, having failed to buy Ferrari, started figuring out how he might steal glory from the dominant Italian firm in the world's most prestigious endurance race—the Le Mans 24 Hour. The next year, in association with the British Lola race car company, a prototype GT was built, and this was dubbed the GT40 due to its 40-inch height. Three cars were entered into Le Mans and despite one of them recording the fastest lap of the race, all three retired, leaving Ferrari to take victory.

Ferrari won again in '65, but Ford persisted and in the '66 race got more than it bargained for by taking first, second and third places. The GT40's winning streak at Le Mans continued for the next three years, powered either by a 425bhp, 302 cubic-inch (4.9-liter) V8 or a 427 cubic-inch (7-liter) V8 producing around 485bhp. The fastest of these race cars could hit a hair-raising 220mph on the 3.5-mile Mulsanne Straight at Le Mans.

In 1967 Ford turned out a detuned, 302 cubic inch road-legal version putting out 335bhp. As a UK press advertisement of the day proclaimed: 'The Ford GT40: £7,540. 0-60mph: 6secs. 1st gear: 58mph.

Top gear: 164mph. Boot space: laughable. Petrol consumption: wicked.' It might have been the price (approx $20,800), trunk space, gas mileage or all three, but the car wasn't a sales success.

The next episode of the GT tale didn't unfold until 36 years later, at the Detroit Auto Show of 2003, with the debut of Ford's GT40 Concept road car. Although bearing an uncanny likeness to the original GT, the Concept was all new and featured an aluminum spaceframe chassis, aluminum body panels and a fiberglass hood. With carbon-fiber used in the aerodynamic underbody and seats, modern weight-saving methods were very much in evidence.

The show car proved such a massive hit that Ford decided to make it into a production model. This would serve as the perfect centerpiece for the company's 100th birthday celebrations in 2004, the same year the first production GTs were delivered to their owners.

Despite being a truly modern supercar, and far more civilized and easier to drive than its ancestor, it follows a very similar formula to the '60s GT40: a powerful mid-mounted V8 clothed in low-slung, race car bodywork (but not quite as low slung as the original—its height is now 44.3 inches, enabling the accommodation of taller drivers). And that 550bhp supercharged 330 cubic-inch (5,410cc) V8 really delivers the goods. The official performance figures from Ford are: 0-100mph in 8.6 seconds, a standing-start quarter-mile time of 11.6secs at a terminal

Customers started taking delivery of the all-new Ford GT (left) in 2004; 2006 saw the introduction of the GTX1 conversion (above) with revised roof system and interior

115

speed of 128mph, and a top speed of 205mph.

American magazine *Car and Driver* recorded a 0-60mph time of just 3.3 seconds, while *Road & Track* managed 0-150mph in 19.5secs and the full mile from a standing start in 29.9secs at 171.4mph. That kind of acceleration is more than enough to scare ordinary mortals, but in true US hot-rodding tradition, Hennessey Performance of Houston, Texas claims its twin-turbocharged conversion can push GT horsepower from 550 to 1,000bhp or more!

But the GT story doesn't end there. With the 1966 Sebring 12hr-winning Ford GTX1 roadster serving as inspiration, Ford unveiled its new GTX1 project at the 2005 SEMA Show in Las Vegas. The X1 roadster conversion became available in 2006 (40 years after that Sebring victory) and features a roof system of four individual hard panels that can be configured as a coupe, T-top, or full convertible, with the panels stowing neatly inside the vehicle.

The GTX1's clamshell engine cover has been redesigned with buttresses flowing from behind the headrests, but there's still a view of the supercharged V8 thru a transparent panel.

The basic X1 conversion includes painting the areas affected by the roof conversion in the original color, while options include different wheels and tires, an interior trim package with special Sparco seats, Brembo two-piece rotors with Brembo logo calipers, adjustable 'coil over' shocks, Borla exhausts and headers, engine performance upgrades, carbon-fiber splitter/diffuser with side spats and the latest 600-watt Sony audio system. The latter allows the transfer of MP3 files from computer to car via a USB cable and its built-in 1GB flash memory holds up to 500 songs.

Technology sure has come a long way since the first Ford GT of 1964, but in the new GT the legend lives on more strongly than ever. ✄

SPECIFICATION	
ENGINE TYPE	V8 supercharged
DISPLACEMENT	330 cu in (5,410cc)
POWER	550bhp @ 6,000rpm
TORQUE	500lb/ft @ 4,500rpm
TRANSMISSION	Six-speed manual
0-60mph	3.3 seconds
TOP SPEED	205mph
PRICE	$153,345 or £120,900. Add $38,000 (£21,650 approx) for optional GTX1 conversion

www.fordvehicles.com, www.gtx1.com

The GT's interior (left) is roomy and well-equipped, with a simple but effective use of materials. The GTX1 (below) offers engine upgrades and the option of open-top motoring

“ Its formula is very similar to the '60s GT40: a powerful ”
mid-mounted V8 clothed in low-slung race car bodywork

"With a 0-60mph time of just 3.3 seconds, the acceleration is more than enough to scare ordinary mortals"

"The Viper is a truly fast car, but if you are very serious about going fast, a Venom could be the one for you "

Hennessey Venom

The Dodge Viper is an American muscle car, world famous for its macho looks and brutal power, but the Venom boosts it to 1,000bhp and takes it one step beyond sanity

What do you get if you take an iconic American sports car, the 510bhp Dodge Viper SRT-10, and almost double its horsepower? Answer: an iconic American supercar with phenomenal performance. A car that can accelerate to 100mph in the time it takes a Porsche Boxster to reach 60mph. A car that can hit 200mph in less time than it takes to read this paragraph out loud.

Getting back to the Venom's source material, the Dodge Viper concept was first unveiled at the 1989 Detroit Auto Show, causing jaws hit the floor in the process. Its macho appearance and 488 cubic inch (8-liter), 400 horsepower V10 motor caused a huge stir and serious enthusiasts couldn't wait to get behind the wheel. In 2002, their patience was rewarded as the concept turned to a production reality and the 160mph Viper hit the streets.

In 1996 the R/T 10, with a removable roof, was joined by the even better-looking GTS hardtop coupe, with power upped from 400 to 450bhp at the same time. Impressive though the Viper still was, it wasn't going to last forever without a thorough makeover, so Dodge asked existing owners what they'd like to see in the next model. Their response was resounding: more power, less weight and keep it raw and free of frills, and when the Viper SRT-10 emerged in 2003, it conformed to their wishes. Displacement was up to 505 cubic inches (8.3 liters), power was up to 500bhp, torque to 525lb/ft, weight was down by 100 pounds (45kg), and it still didn't

have such frills as cruise control or cup holders.

Then, for 2006, further improvements were made. A hardtop coupe SRT-10 joined the existing convertible, while horsepower and torque rose again, this time to 510bhp and 535lb/ft. The Viper's brakes were improved, too. Stopping power came from 14-inch brake rotors gripped by huge Brembo calipers front and rear. This resulted in braking performance of 60-0mph in less than 100 feet and contributes toward a 0-100-0mph time in the mid-12-seconds bracket. Viper SRT-10 performance was further assisted by a speed-sensing limited-slip differential, race-bred independent suspension made from aluminum, forged and polished aluminum wheels (18 x 10-inch front, 19 x 13-inch rear) and Michelin run-flat tires with pressure sensors.

A Viper of any vintage is a truly fast car, but the '06 SRT-10 pushes the boundaries even further with a sub-4-second zero-to-sixty and a 190mph top speed. However, that's not where this story ends. Enter the Hennessey Venom 1000 Twin Turbo…

Houston, Texas is the home town of Hennessey Performance Engineering, the home of the world's quickest, fastest and most powerful Vipers. For 2006 Hennessey plans to build just 24 of these hot-rods, and if you've the best part of a quarter of a million

The 2006 Viper SRT-10 (left) is a serious beast with 510bhp, but the Hennessey Venom (right and above) nearly doubles that horsepower thanks to twin turbos

bucks and are very serious about going fast, a Venom could be the car for you. As you can see from the specification box on the right, the Venom makes a truly sinful 1,000bhp and 1,100lb/ft, so here's a brief account of what transforms a Viper into a Venom and what it can do.

First, take an '06 Viper SRT-10 and stroke the V10 motor to 522 cubic inches (8,557cc). Also lower the compression from 9.6:1 to 9.0:1 and instal a pair of Garrett turbochargers and an intercooler. Fit a front airdam, rear diffuser and spoiler. Upgrade suspension units and lower ride height. Instal even beefier Brembo brakes, adjustable traction control and a Quaiffe 'Extreme-Duty' differential. Bolt on Venom 7R forged aluminum wheels (19 x 10-inch front, 20 x 13-inch rear) with Michelin Pilot Sport 2 tires. Then trim the interior in Connolly leather, put in 5-point racing harnesses and finally, should you find yourself going so fast that you lose track of which state or country you're in, instal a DVD navigation system in the dashboard.

So how fast is Venom fast? Well, Hennessey claims 0-60mph in 2.9 seconds, 0-100mph in 5.9secs, 0-150mph in 10.9secs, 0-200mph in 19.9secs and a top speed of 255mph. If those figures seem a little too breathtaking, American car magazine *Road & Track* took a customer's Venom 1000 to an airfield runway and achieved 0-60mph in 3.6secs, 0-100 in 6.8, 0-150 in 11.5 and 0-200 in 21.3.

Along the way, the Venom covered the standing quarter-mile in 11.0secs at 145.5mph, the standing half-mile in 16.5secs at 178.1mph and charged on to cover a full mile in 25.6secs at 210.2mph before the driver had to hit the brakes while still accelerating hard. At 220mph, he would have had to change from fifth to sixth gear...

A max speed of 255mph? Probably. An ultimate American supercar? Definitely. ▨

SPECIFICATION	
ENGINE TYPE	V10 turbocharged
DISPLACEMENT	522 cu in (8,557cc)
POWER	1,000bhp @ 5,000rpm
TORQUE	1,100lb/ft @ 3,800rpm
TRANSMISSION	Six-speed manual
0-60mph	2.9 seconds (see text)
TOP SPEED	255mph (see text)
PRICE	$225,000
	(£128,000 approx)
www.hennesseyperformance.com	

The Viper SRT-10 interior (below) is re-trimmed in Connolly leather by Hennessey for the Venom. Racing harnesses and a DVD navigation system are also fitted

"The MT900S surely offers the ultimate in driving excitement"

Mosler
MT900S

Developed as the road-going version of a Le Mans race car, the Mosler is a true transatlantic collaboration. The company is American-owned, but the car is built in the UK

In the world of supercars, the name Mosler isn't quite as well known as, say, Ferrari or Porsche. But the company's owner, American entrepreneur and financier Warren Mosler, states that: "Our mission is to offer the top performance sports car capable of the lowest track lap times that is legal for US roads".

That's a brave claim, considering that in standard trim the Corvette ZO6-powered Mosler MT900S makes less horsepower than every other supercar in this book, and in three cases less than half as much power. The Mosler is also less powerful than all the GTs, convertibles, sedans and concepts, in fact, every other car here bar three of the five SUVs.

But the Mosler's here for a reason. It has an ace up its sleeve—at just 2,144 pounds (972.5kg) it weighs considerably less than every other car on these pages. And, having 435bhp on tap (in base model spec) coupled with the subtle but significant advantages that low weight gives, the Mosler is in fact a car capable of very serious performance. On a power-to-weight basis, its 447bhp per tonne trumps quite a few Ferraris—the F40, F50, F430 and new Enzo-powered 620hp 599 GTB, to name but a few, plus every Lamborghini up to and including the new 640hp Murciélago LP640.

So what exactly is a Mosler MT900S? Put simply, it's a road-going version of the successful MT900R

Right: the Mosler packs a mid-mounted Corvette V8 engine, with the option of three different power ratings: 435, 540 or 600bhp. Below: the road car's interior is simple, but not as spartan as the race car

With an advanced composite monocoque chassis made from carbon-fiber and carbon-aluminum honeycomb, the MT900S is every inch the road-legal race car

racer that is being manufactured in limited numbers for the street to qualify the race car for entry in the 2007 Le Mans 24 Hour race.

Though Mosler HQ is located in Florida, the car is assembled in the UK, and the core of the MT900S is its advanced composite monocoque chassis made from carbon-fiber and carbon-aluminum honeycomb. Substantial carbon-fiber sills and central spars, along with the structural carbon front and rear bulkheads, roof and A-pillars, create an ultra-strong, ultra-lightweight cockpit. Chrome-molybdenum steel sub-frames provide the mountings for the steering, suspension, engine and transaxle.

A mid-mounted 346 cubic-inch (5,672cc) Corvette LS6 V8 motor provides power, but a 427 cubic-inch (7-liter) V8 with 540bhp and 540lb/ft of torque is also available, as is a supercharged, 600bhp version of the smaller V8. The power is transmitted via an inverted Porsche GT3 6-speed manual gearbox and transaxle and a limited-slip differential.

Suspension is double wishbones all round, with Penske 3-way adjustable 'coil over' units combined with adjustable anti-roll bars. Corvette aluminum uprights hold the hubs and wheels in place, while the steering (which can be specified in left or right-hand-drive) is non-power-assisted.

For the US market, the car is fitted as standard with Corvette brakes for easy servicing, but the European-spec Mosler comes with 355mm (14-inch) diameter grooved, drilled and ventilated floating rotors, with 6-piston Wilwood alloy calipers at front and rear. The MT900S rolls on OZ forged aluminum alloy 3-piece wheels (19-inch front, 20-inch rear) fitted with Dunlop SP9000 Sport tires. Michelin Pilot Sport 2 tires are optional. The rear body section provides a location for the standard-fit, adjustable carbon-fiber rear wing, and this panel can be lifted up to reveal enough luggage space for two people.

An MT900S in Photon spec boasts a Hewland sequential transmission, carbon-fiber seats, 18-inch carbon-fiber wheels with Hoosier tires, alternative 3-way adjustable damper units with titanium springs plus a lightweight exhaust, battery, alternator and air-conditioner unit.

On paper this all looks very impressive and, you've guessed it, it works pretty well on the road, too. In a road test conducted in 2003 by the US car magazine *Motor Trend*, a 346 cubic-inch, 435bhp

MT900S Photon clocked these times: 0-60mph in 3.13 seconds, 0-100mph in 7.11secs, the standing quarter in 11.02secs at 126.88mph, and the standing mile in 30.4secs at 154.3mph. Its braking was no less spectacular, pulling off the 0-100-0mph test in just 10.98secs. Other cars on that same test included a Lamborghini Murciélago, a Ferrari 575M and a Viper SRT-10 and, although the Viper narrowly out-braked the Mosler, the MT900S beat all-comers on the 600 foot (183 meter) slalom and the 1,700 foot (518 meter) figure-of-eight course.

True, the MT900S did lose out to the Murciélago, the Viper and the 575M on top speed (on a 5-mile oval circuit), but either of the more powerful engine options would doubtless have put the Mosler right back in the frame.

The Mosler may not be the best known, the most powerful or expensive supercar, and it doesn't have the heritage or history of other marques, but it surely offers the ultimate in driving excitement. ✳

SPECIFICATION	
ENGINE TYPE	V8 (supercharger optional)
DISPLACEMENT	346 cu in (5,672cc) (see text)
POWER	435bhp @ 6,000rpm (see text)
TORQUE	400lb/ft @ 4,800rpm (see text)
TRANSMISSION	Six-speed manual
0-60mph	3.1 seconds
TOP SPEED	190mph-plus
PRICE	$210,000 (£120,000 approx)
www.moslerauto.com	

The Mosler's rear body section, with its adjustable carbon-fiber wing, is removable, allowing access to luggage space for two people

" Every inch a true supercar,
right down to its half-million-
dollar-plus price tag "

Saleen S7 Twin Turbo

The single-minded pursuit of performance and luxury is what enables the Saleen to take on the top supercars

Sometimes a manufacturer states its case pretty clearly. So, to quote Saleen's own words: 'The Saleen S7 Twin Turbo is designed to compete with the fastest, quickest, best-handling and most luxurious cars in the world, while providing a distinctly American driving experience for the fortunate few who will own one'.

It's hard to argue with that statement, as the S7 Twin Turbo is every inch a true supercar, right down to its half-million-dollar-plus price tag. It is a further development of the original S7 model, which the Californian company first revealed at the Laguna Seca raceway in the summer of 2000.

It had a mid-mounted 427 cubic-inch (7-liter) V8 that produced up to 550 horsepower with 525lb/ft of torque. Weighing in at 2,750 pounds (1,247kg) the S7 boasted a very competitive power-to-weight ratio of 441bhp per tonne. Along with its 41-inch (104cm) high, low-drag race car body, this translated into a 0-60mph time of 3.9 seconds, 0-100 in 7.7secs, the standing quarter in 11.8secs at 127mph and a top speed of around the 200mph mark.

When it went on sale in 2002, the S7 was the only street-legal car in the USA with more than

500bhp and 500lb/ft of torque. Trouble was, Saleen barely had time to rest on its laurels before a whole new rash of even more exotic supercars came to the market, all touting power figures that were well above the once-magic level of 500 horsepower.

Although already occupied with maintaining its reputation as a regular manufacturers' champion in GT sports car racing with its S7R racer, to stay in the street legal supercar game Saleen had to act. Fortunately, its engineers had anticipated this on-slaught of horsepower from Italy and Germany, so for the second edition S7 they were ready with a pair of water-cooled Saleen-Garrett turbochargers.

With the redline set at 6,500rpm, plus stainless steel valves, titanium retainers, beryllium exhaust valve seats, an aluminum throttle body, redesigned

Top: The S7's chassis is a high-tech combination of spaceframe chassis backed up with honeycomb composite reinforcement for maximum lightness and rigidity

" The carbon-fiber body "
contributes to the car's
overall structure and rigidity

cylinder heads and a stainless steel exhaust, the new Twin Turbo has 200 extra brake horsepower and an additional 175ft/lb of torque. All this equates to a power-to-weight figure of 561bhp per tonne, which betters the Ferrari Enzo and the McLaren F1.

The S7 in either guise features a spaceframe chassis to which honeycomb composite reinforcing is grafted, while its carbon-fiber body contributes to the car's overall structure and rigidity. Suspension is dealt with by fully independent double wishbones with 'coil over' springs and aluminum dampers front and rear, while the uprights at each corner are made from machined aluminum.

A major improvement in ride was achieved for the 2005 Twin Turbo model, with the use of dual-stage coil springs. The first spring has a lower rate than the single springs fitted to the first S7, and so gives a softer ride during normal street driving. But this is a flat-bottomed car producing aerodynamic downforce, so the faster you go, the more downforce the car develops. On the new car a second, stiffer spring starts coming into play at around about the 100mph mark, when the car begins to develop heavy-duty downforce.

The Saleen handles like a racer, but to slow things down to cornering speed it needs a high-end braking system. So Brembo aluminum six-piston calipers are fitted, with huge vented discs front and rear, while Saleen-designed forged aluminum alloy wheels feature auto-locking center wheel nuts and wear Michelin Pilot Sport 2 rubber.

The S7 Twin Turbo's body has redesigned front and rear diffusers, which along with a new rear spoiler have cleverly yielded a 40% reduction in aerodynamic drag and a 60% increase in downforce. For convenience, there is front and rear stowage with fitted luggage and, in true supercar style, the doors open up and away from the body.

Inside, the S7 features asymmetrical seating, with the driver being positioned slightly closer to the car's centerline than the passenger. This improves ergonomics for the driver, as well as lateral weight distribution. With custom-fitted seating (and a fully-adjustable steering wheel and pedals) the S7 can take drivers up six feet six inches tall. The seats and interior surfaces are covered in leather and suede, which form part of a long list of interior creature comforts that even includes a rear-view video camera.

But the bottom line for a supercar is performance. In that respect, Saleen's figures for the S7 Twin Turbo are: 0-60mph in 2.8 seconds, 0-100 in 6.0, a standing quarter-mile in 10.7secs at 136mph, 0-100-0mph in 10.9secs and a maximum speed of around 235mph. That certainly puts it right up there with fastest, quickest cars in the world. ▨

With custom-fitted seating, plus an adjustable steering wheel and pedals, the S7 can make drivers of up to six feet six inches comfortable

SPECIFICATION	
ENGINE TYPE	V8 turbocharged
DISPLACEMENT	427 cu in (7,004cc)
POWER	750bhp @ 6,300rpm
TORQUE	700lb/ft @ 4,800rpm
TRANSMISSION	Six-speed manual
0-60mph	2.8 seconds
TOP SPEED	235mph
PRICE	$555,000
	(£319,300 approx)
www.saleen.com	

“The most powerful
production road car
ever, in any book”

S S C Ultimate Aero

Searching for the most powerful car in this whole collection of awesome automobiles? Well stop right here. This is a machine which takes performance to unbelievable levels. So exactly how many bangs and how many bucks? Read on…

The SSC Ultimate Aero not only kicks out more horsepower than any other car in this book, it is also the most powerful production road car ever to feature in any book.

The Ultimate Aero pumps out an eye-popping 1,046 horsepower, giving it a genuine claim to the title of most powerful factory-assembled road car in the history of the internal combustion engine.

And what an engine this is. An all-American, all-aluminum 387 cubic-inch Corvette V8 gives this beast its bite, with the help of a supercharger and some heavy tuning. Slung under a slippery-shaped carbon-fiber composite body weighing just 135lb, with a drag coefficient of just 0.357, this power unit's incredible output can push the Ultimate Aero through the air with brain-scrambling speed.

So just how fast is it? You'd expect the Ultimate Aero's top speed to be unbelievable, but it's time to recalibrate your brain, and while you're at it take a seat, because you're in for a shock.

So far, the Ultimate Aero has hardly broken sweat. It has cruised around the Pocono race track in Pennsylvania at 'around 210mph', but calculations from wind tunnel tests with a real full-size car have revealed its true potential top speed. The result was a projected maximum of between 260 and 273mph.

Yes, you read that correctly: two hundred and sixty to two hundred and seventy three miles per hour.

Acceleration is in the realms of dragstrip dreams, with the potential to beat all-comers away from the stop lights. At the time of writing, no performance test figures for the Ultimate Aero have been posted, but the $240,000 'standard' Aero has been tested. This 'base model' comes fully loaded with power

The looks are very Lamborghini. But no Lambo road car ever boasted such an incredible amount of horsepower. The Ultimate Aero packs over 1,000bhp

In tests at Pocono race track, Pennsylvania, the Ultimate Aero hit 210mph, but the car's makers say there's plenty more to come yet...

windows, DVD navigation, 10-speaker audio system, a reversing camera and a luxurious leather interior. But even with all that weighty equipment it can still sprint from 0-60mph in 2.94 seconds, blitz from 0-100mph and back down to zero in 11.8 seconds, charge to a 10.44-second standing quarter-mile and hit an estimated top speed of 249mph.

That's all from the standard Aero's 787bhp and 689lb/ft of torque. Compare that with the Ultimate Aero's 1,046bhp and 821lb/ft, and dial in the fact that, at 2,650lb (1,202kg) it's 200lb (91kg) lighter than the standard car, and you get the idea – only the very brave and the very talented will ever get to feel the full, terrifying force of its performance.

Anyone keen to taste the exclusivity of owning an Ultimate Aero will also have to be very rich. It's a rare car with a rare price, unless $654,500 (£370,500 approx) is just loose change to you. At the time of writing, only one Ultimate Aero has been built, but SSC Autos plans on being able to satisfy customer demand for up to two dozen of these hypercars.

Shelby Super Cars' founder and lead designer Jerod Shelby (no relation to famous American racer and performance car builder Carroll Shelby) first unveiled the original Aero SC/8T in Monterey back in 2004. There's no doubt the body styling bears more than a passing resemblance to a Lamborghini Diablo, especially its vertically-opening doors, but the Ultimate Aero's have an extra trick. They rise up with air pressure assistance and then gently close again when the pressure is released.

Once behind the wheel, it's unusually spacious compared to the Diablo. Several pro baseball players gave the interior an impromptu try-out during the car's Pocono test session, and discovered that it could comfortably accommodate adults up to 6' 6" (1.98m) and weighing 300lbs (136kg).

Despite SSC's declared intention to build the world's fastest road car, there's no confirmed data yet on the Ultimate Aero's top speed. A Bonneville Speed Week shoot-out between the supercar makers currently vying for the max speed crown—Bugatti, Hennessey, Koenigsegg and SSC—would be the ideal way to find out which is top dog. It probably won't ever happen, but boy do we wish it would... ✂

SPECIFICATION	
ENGINE TYPE	V8, supercharged
DISPLACEMENT	387.2 cu in (6,348cc)
POWER	1,046bhp @ 6,950rpm
TORQUE	821lb/ft @ 6,200rpm
TRANSMISSION	n/a
0-60mph	Under 2.9secs
TOP SPEED	260-273mph (claimed)
PRICE	$654,500 (£370,500 approx)
www.sscautos.com	

The Aero shows off its gullwing doors which rise vertically with air-pressure assistance

Concept Cars

A car born of a notion, idea or plan, but not in current production. Built for experimentation and evaluation purposes, and to gauge public opinion. Concepts sometimes reappear as production models.

Aston Martin Rapide

Holden Efijy

Lamborghini Concept S

Maserati Birdcage 75th

Maybach Exelero

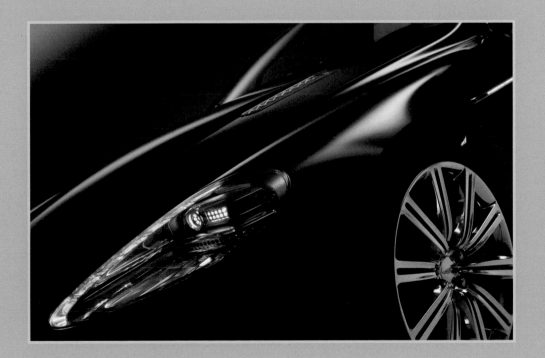

" Even more painfully gorgeous than the **"**
company's DB9 and Vanquish models

Aston Martin Rapide

Many concept cars are wild flights of fantasy with little chance of making it into production. But not this one, it's a close representation of an upcoming Aston four-door car

As if the stunning DB9 and Vanquish models didn't already provide enough temptation, at the 2006 Detroit Auto Show Aston Martin unleashed something even more painfully gorgeous. Called the Rapide, this fully-functioning concept car is a pretty accurate and mouthwatering taster of how Aston's forthcoming four-door car will turn out, both visually and mechanically.

Although the company is far better known for a series of beautiful two-door GT cars dating back to the early 1950s, the Rapide is by no means the first four-door car Aston Martin has produced, and nor does it represent the first use of the Rapide name.

At the 1927 London Olympia Motor Show Aston Martin displayed a hardtop tourer that sported long, flowing lines and sat close to the ground. Four years later, another four-door saloon was exhibited and it featured intriguing touches like an opening glass panel above the rear passenger compartment.

Soon after World War II, the British manufacturer Lagonda was bought by David Brown, the man who was to give his initials to the famous 'DB' series of Aston Martins which continue to this day. Brown also bought Aston Martin and merged the two companies in 1948, but 14 years prior to this Lagonda had launched the very sporting 4.5-liter Rapide model at the London Motor Show.

In the decades following the war, the David Brown Astons helped to create the quintessential

image of the two-door, four-seater GT. In the 1970s and '80s, Aston Martin built four-door variants of the V8 and Virage models for select customers. But the most memorable four-door of this period was the 'Lagonda' launched at the London Earls Court Show in 1976. Powered by a 340bhp, 5,340cc (326 cu in) V8, its stunning, razor-edged exterior and luxury sci-fi interior tempted no less than 170 show goers into placing a deposit on the exotic £10,000 ($18,000) car. Such was the 140mph Lagonda's appeal that, by the time first deliveries of the car were made three years later, the price had risen to an even more exotic £32,000 ($67,800), but customers still willingly paid up.

Like most Aston Martins past and present, the new Rapide is an energetic performer. Powered by the V12 engine from the DB9, but uprated from 450bhp to 480bhp, the car's performance is on a par with the DB9 (0-60mph in 4.9 seconds and a 186mph top speed) although the Rapide's gearing has been adjusted to suit its longer wheelbase and more refined ride.

At five meters (16.4ft) long, the Rapide is 30cm (11.8 inches) longer than a DB9 but only 140kg (309lb)

Traditional Aston Martin qualities, such as hand-built construction (top) and high performance from a 6-liter V12 engine (right) combine with modern high-tech gadgetry and communication systems (above, centre)

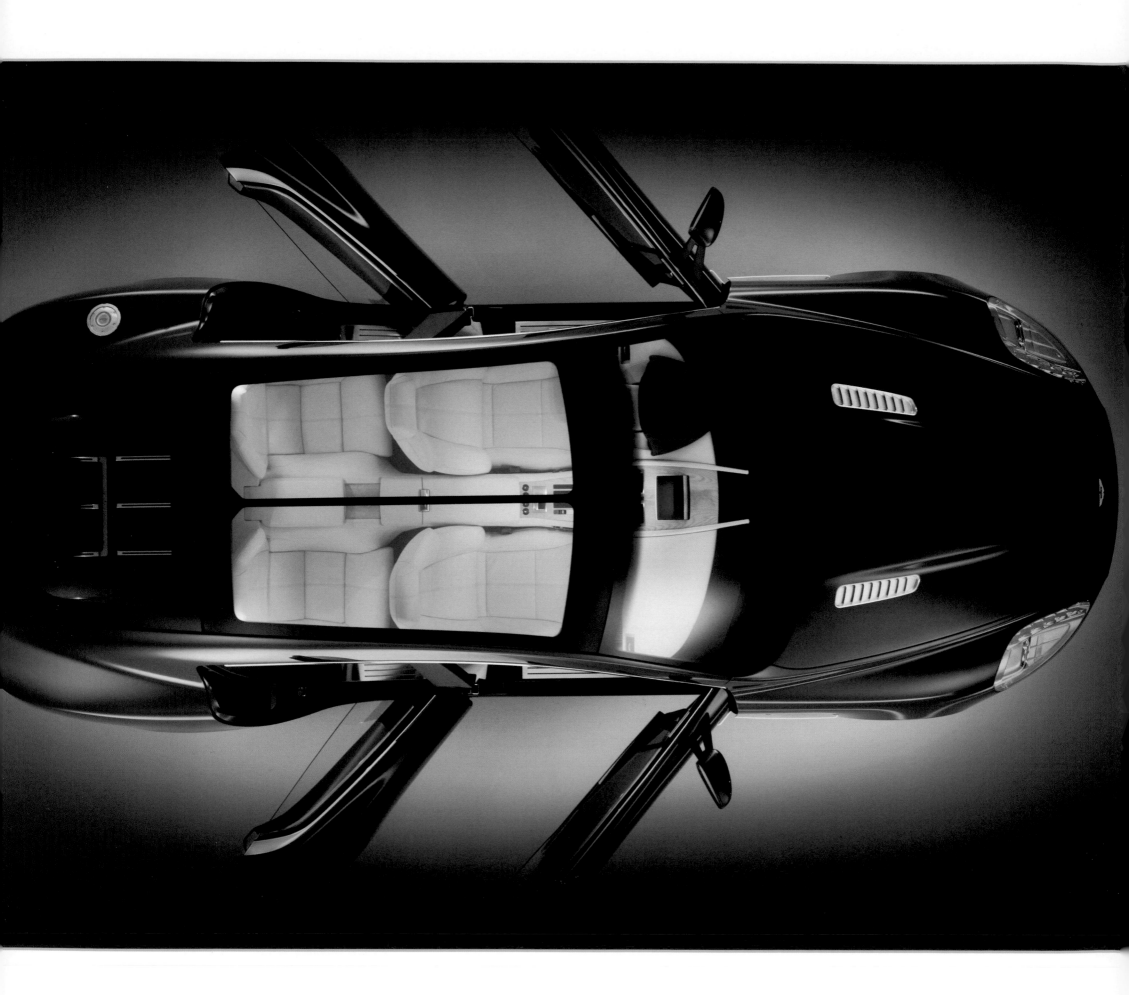

heavier. Carbon brakes and calipers, a first for Aston Martin, give the Rapide immense stopping power.

In the words of Aston's Design Director Marek Reichman: "We wanted to make the most beautiful four-door car in the world". In particular, he highlights the "beautiful harmony" of the line that runs through the Rapide's bodywork, giving the car the appearance of motion even while stationary.

"It's not a wedge, it's graceful and flowing," adds Reichman. "We decided to let the lines flow right through the body to the tail, which ends very beautifully. Although the Rapide is just 4 centimeters (1.6in) taller than the DB9, the proportion of the cabin section is the same, allowing the flowing lines to encase a spacious passenger compartment."

The Rapide's interior is an exquisite leather-swathed environment with custom-embossed hide, extensive interior storage space and 'mood lighting' to maximise both spaciousness and ambience. Wood is used for its structural properties and appearance,

as are aluminium and glass, with carbon-fiber utilized for its strength and weight-saving properties and not just to create a showy finish. A transparent polycarbonate roof gives the cabin a light an airy feel, bringing an increased sense of spatial awareness for the passengers. The cars luxuriously-appointed rear seats have their own DVD screens as well as controls for the audio and climate systems.

Access to the generous rear luggage compartment is thru a hatchback, a practical feature also found on the pioneering Aston Martin DB2/4 of 1952. Each rear seat also folds down individually, while the Rapide's trunk features a chiller cabinet in the boot that contains a magnum of champagne along with four elegant flutes to drink it from.

But most important is the Rapide's sheer beauty. With this in mind, the last word must go to Aston Martin boss Dr Ulrich Bez: "Proportions must be perfect. If we hadn't been able to achieve this, then we would not have built the car." ▨

SPECIFICATION	
ENGINE TYPE	V12
DISPLACEMENT	5,935cc (362 cu in)
POWER	480bhp @ c.6,000rpm
TORQUE	n/a
TRANSMISSION	Six-speed 'Touchtronic' manual
0-62mph	4.9 seconds approx
TOP SPEED	186mph approx
PRICE	It's not for sale, sir
www.astonmartin.com	

Below: four doors and a hatchback give a high level of practicality to back up the car's sheer beauty. Left: the transparent polycarbonate roof floods the cabin with light and enables the passengers to stargaze at night time

" The Efijy represents flamboyance and "
design decadence taken to the limit

Holden Efijy

For sheer show-stopping Wow! factor, the Efijy is a hard act to beat. Inspired by the ornate curves of '40s and '50s automobiles, this Australian one-off is a real retro dream

*I*f there's a prize for sheer voluptuousness, for flamboyance and for design decadence taken to the limit, then it has to go to Holden's truly fabulous Efijy. First shown in Sydney, Australia in late 2005, the Efijy is a radical, retro custom coupe concept with supercharged V8 power, a lengthened Corvette chassis and state-of-the-art technology and gizmology throughout.

The Efijy (pronounced eff-ij-ee) is not intended for production, sadly. It was a fun project intended to showcase the talents of General Motors' Holden design team. It will come as no surprise that Holden Chief Designer and Efijy project leader Richard Ferlazzo is a long-time custom car fanatic. He started sketching the first designs for this showmobile back in 1989 and confesses that the car exists "purely for automotive entertainment".

Ferlazzo explains the inspiration for this automotive art-throb in these terms: "The Efijy is our accolade to the talented designers who cut loose with some fantastically flamboyant styling in the 1940s and 1950s". But the Efijy also owes much, not least its cleverly contrived name, to the much less glamorous Holden FJ, an affordable popular vehicle sold to the Australian public in the mid-1950s.

The FJ was available in standard sedan, business sedan, special sedan, panel van or utility/pick-up form. Almost 170,000 were produced from 1953 to 1956 and they sold for around 2,000 Australian dollars

Below: supercharged V8 develops 645bhp. Right: the interior has many retro touches, including body-coloured metal dashboard and Bakelite-style push-button controls

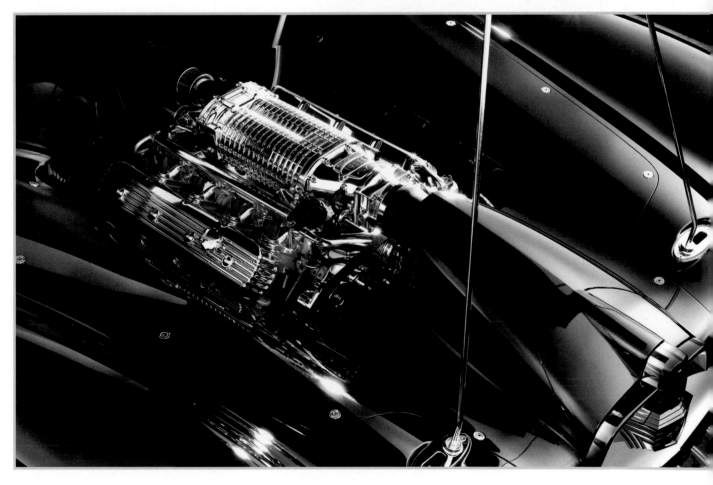

(about £800 or $2,240 US) powered by a 2.15-liter (132 cubic inch) six-cylinder motor with 60bhp.

You'll not be surprised to learn that the 2005 Efijy is a little more powerful than that. In fact, it's almost 11 times more powerful. Its 'Vortec LS2' motor, an all-aluminum, fourth-generation version of GM's timeless small-block V8, has a 6-liter (366 cubic-inch) capacity and, with a Roots-type supercharger, pumps out 645bhp and 560lb/ft of torque.

The Efijy's monster motor is mated to a rear-mounted 4-speed automatic transmission with push button electronic control. Power is then transferred via a limited-slip differential to massive 22 x 10-inch billet aluminum wheels with fluting which echoes the old FJ's more modest 15 x 4-inch wheels.

Reflecting its street-sled heritage, the Efijy's front wheels are 20 x 9-inch, while the brakes feature 381mm (15-inch) grooved and ventilated rotors (front and rear) with six-piston aluminum calipers (front) and four-piston aluminum calipers (rear). The exhaust is a dual 2.5-inch (635mm) stainless system with custom headers and billet aluminum tailpipes.

The aggressive, FJ-inspired grille looms larger than life, and this fronts a wickedly curvaceous glass-fiber body. A Corvette rolling chassis was lengthened to accommodate the Efijy's 17-feet (5.2 meters) long

pillarless design. The 'Soprano Purple' paint has multiple layers of translucent pigmented topcoats, and all the metal brightwork is hand-made from billet aluminum. A proximity sensor opens the driver's door automatically as the driver approaches, and this fully reveals the Efijy's tombstone-shaped, deep cream leather bucket seats with integral belts.

The drop-down, touch-control LCD screen and instrument cluster (glowing with the number '53', another FJ gesture) are set into the body-colored metal dash and pulsate with a 1950s radiogram-style orange glow. The push-button controls for the electronic auto transmission have a pearlescent, Bakelite appearance, while the floor is finished in figured maple timber veneer with aluminum inserts.

The car's low-rider stance can be accentuated by adjustable air suspension. At the touch of an LCD screen, it can hunker down to just 1.06 inches (27mm) of ground clearance, or pump itself back up to a more practical driving height.

The use of high-intensity LED headlights and tail lights is echoed by LED lighting inside, including the courtesy and sill illumination lamps, and several of these are dual filament so they can throw different colors depending on the application. The Efijy is also equipped with a cutting-edge in-car entertainment

system and features hard drive audio/video storage with a robust amplifier and speaker systems.

Advanced designs and clay models for the Efijy were prepared during 2003, but Holden then had to put Efijy plans on hold to work on more practical but much less dramatic concept cars. But, as things turned out, a couple of years here or there didn't matter a great deal, as this is a car that will have just as much impact in 2103.

SPECIFICATION	
ENGINE TYPE	V8 supercharged
DISPLACEMENT	366 cubic inches (6.0 liters)
POWER	645bhp @ 6,400rpm
TORQUE	560lb/ft @ 4,200rpm
TRANSMISSION	Four-speed electronic auto
0-62mph	4.0 seconds (estimated)
TOP SPEED	180mph (estimated)
PRICE	Sorry, you can't buy it
www.holden.com.au	

The name 'Efijy' is an adaptation of the word 'effigy', meaning 'a stylish representation of something famous

"The two distinct compartments lend the car an aggressive, futuristic Batmobile look"

Lamborghini
Concept S

Lamborghini are famous for producing wild-looking cars, but it's unlikely the Italian company will put this particular one into production. Unless we all wish very, very hard...

An international jury comprising designers, automobile historians, art experts and journalists which assembled a while back in Milan, Italy, voted the Lamborghini Gallardo as 'The world's most beautiful car in 2003' in the sport and supercar category. Now you may not agree with the jury's verdict, but you'd be on thin ice if you tried to argue that the Gallardo was anything other than utterly stunning.

But Lamborghini's designers allowed themselves little time for self-congratulation, because just a few years later, at the 2005 Geneva Motorshow, the Concept S design study was revealed. This 'extreme and spectacular expression of the 'Lamborghini brand', created by Luc Donckerwolke and his design team in Lamborghini's hometown of Sant' Agata, was said to have been inspired by the classic 'mono-posto' single-seater racing cars of the past.

Substantial public interest at the Geneva Show prompted Lamborghini to build a driveable proto-type to further gauge potential customer demand, and a running Concept S was duly shown later in the year at the Monterey Concorso Italiano and the Pebble Beach Concours d'Elegance in the USA.

This Concept S prototype differed very little from the original Geneva design study. The pair of low, extremely sleek windshields, which echo the low, wrap-around perspex screens used by the single-seater racers of old, were re-designed for homologation reasons, but the car (as shown here)

looks even more extreme than the original. In the 'Concept S', these heavily-tinted screens divide the driver and passenger 'cockpit' into two distinct compartments, which lends the car an aggressive, futuristic Batmobile look.

This space between the occupants also directs air toward an additional engine air intake positioned just behind the seats, also allowing an electronically controlled and retractable rear-view mirror to be mounted centrally, to allow an unobstructed view of what's behind the car. Concept S aerodynamics were further optimized with the addition of front and rear spoilers and a large rear diffuser.

As the Concept S is based on the Gallardo, its chassis is an aluminum spaceframe clothed in largely aluminum bodywork. Suspension is by aluminum double wishbones at front and rear, self-adjusting dampers, plus anti-roll, anti-dive and anti-squat systems. Braking is dealt with by 8-piston (front) and 4-piston (rear) aluminum alloy callipers with 365mm/335mm ventilated rotors, while wheels are 19-inch aluminum alloys wearing Pirelli P Zero tires.

The 'Concept S' Gallardo V10 engine has 40 valves with variable intake geometry and produces 494bhp with 376bl/ft of torque. This is fed through either a 6-speed manual or E-gear manual paddle-shift transmission to a permanent 4-wheel-drive system. Performance for the hardtop Gallardo is quoted as 0-62mph in 4.2secs with a 192mph max.

At the time of writing, there is still no official word as to whether the Concept S will ever make it to production-model status, but it's pretty unlikely,

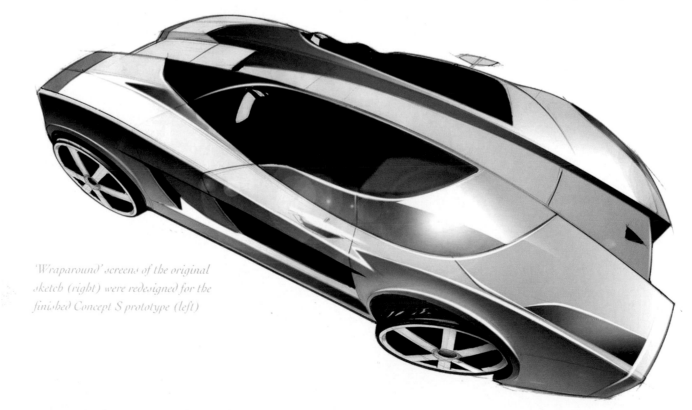

'Wraparound' screens of the original sketch (right) were redesigned for the finished Concept S prototype (left)

not least because the car doesn't have any kind of roof. The structure would also provide inadequate protection in a roll-over accident or in the rain. So, for those who want the wind in their hair and are prepared to settle for something similar, there is now the Gallardo Spyder.

Launched at the Frankfurt Motor Show in the fall of 2005, the Gallardo Spyder has an electronically controlled cloth hood that resides, when lowered, beneath a carbon-fiber cover. The whole raising and lowering operation takes only 20 seconds and the Spyder's rear screen moves automatically while the roof is being opened or closed. The driver can choose to have the screen remain in the lowered position by pressing the appropriate button. There is also a function that positions the roof to allow access to the engine bay.

The Spyder also features a few modifications from the original Gallardo engine and transmission. Its V10 motor develops more power—512bhp at 8,000rpm—and its 6-speed gearbox features lower ratios. Both of these factors combine to give a top speed of 195mph (with the roof up), 191mph (with the roof down) and the 0-62mph sprint in 4.3 seconds. The Spyder's steering is also more direct and precise than the hardtop model, and also has recalibrated suspension.

This is all well and good but, unfortunately, the production Spyder doesn't look quite as amazing as the Concept S. Also unfortunate is that the one-off Concept S will probably remain as just a one-off. It will therefore be remembered, like the one and only 1968 Lamborghini Miura Roadster, as one of the rarest and best looking cars ever built. ▨

SPECIFICATION	
ENGINE TYPE	V10
DISPLACEMENT	4,961cc (303 cu in)
POWER	494bhp @ 7,800rpm
TORQUE	376lb/ft @ 4,500rpm
TRANSMISSION	Six-speed 'E-gear' paddle shift manual, 4WD
0-62mph	4.3 seconds (estimated)
TOP SPEED	190mph (estimated)
PRICE	Priceless
www.lamborghini.com	

The lack of roof or rollover structure means the outrageous Concept S (left) will probably never make production. So the new Gallardo Spyder (below) will just have to do...

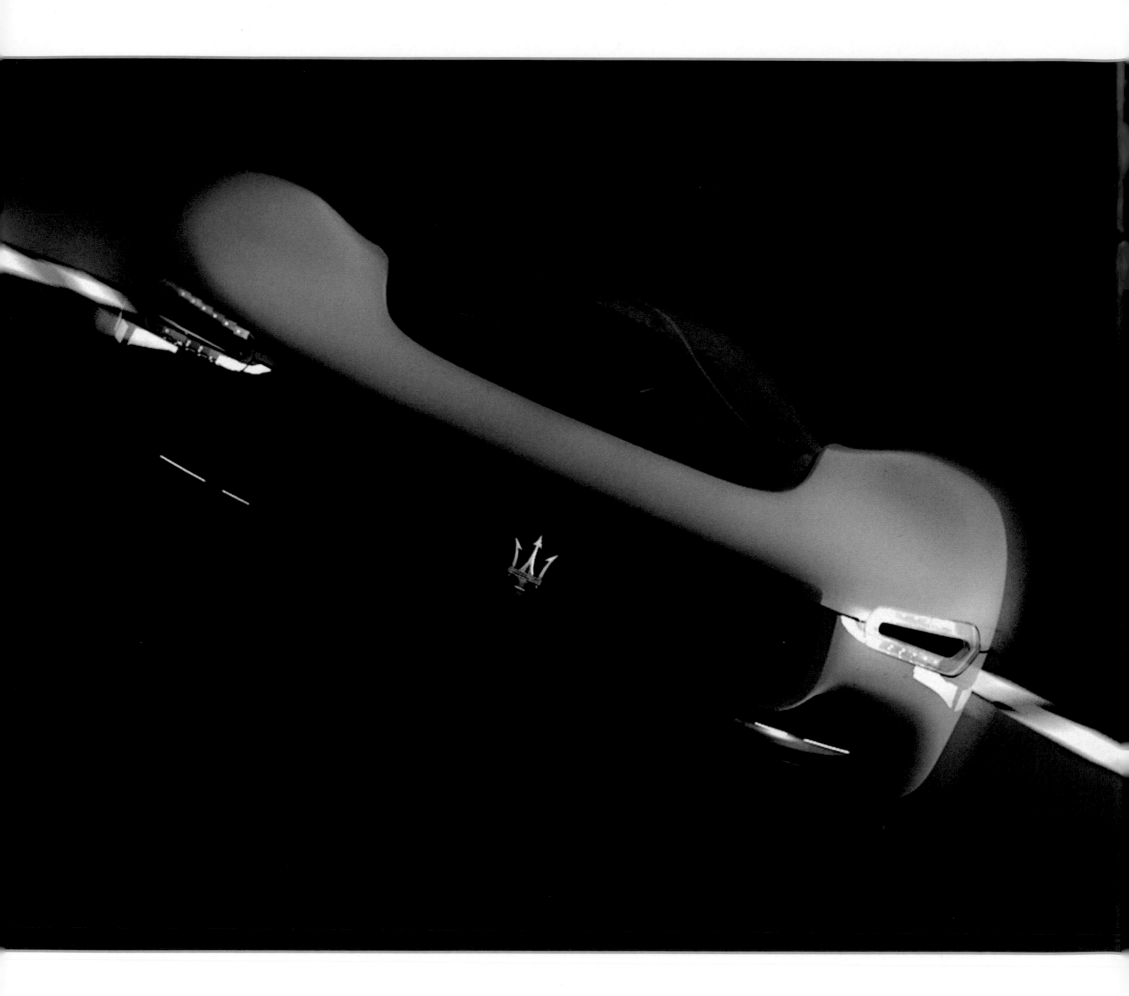

Maserati
Birdcage 75th

It looks more like a piece of futuristic sculpture than an automobile, and the creators of the stunning Birdcage 75th regard it as a work of art, too. It could only be Italian

There's no doubting that the Italians have a way with clothes, food, motorcycles and cars, but they have a way with words, too. Here's how Italian manufacturer Maserati describes this car: 'The Birdcage 75th is built in homage to the spirit of the dream car era and is based on the road/racing carbon-fiber chassis of the Maserati MC12. It seeks to capture the ultimate expression of speed, sensuality and elegance—to create a functional and dynamic automotive sculpture.'

Quite so, but more simply this is one seriously cool car. And, as you are no doubt wondering, it is called the 75th to celebrate the 75th anniversary of

the world famous design house Pininfarina, the firm responsible for the design of this car. While the main object was to extend the boundaries of supercar styling, its V12 engine which packs over 50bhp more than the standard 624bhp MC12 meant that the design had to be more than just super-pretty,—it had to be strong, purposeful and super-effective.

Pininfarina's first task was to re-body (in carbon-fiber) the mechanicals in the most efficient manner possible, but in a way that didn't look like it was a clone of any existing model. This was no easy task, considering that the glamorous MC12, as well as Ferrari's Enzo and FXX, (all of which share similar

chassis and mechanicals), were already out there.

Pininfarina decided on a central teardrop shape to encapsulate the passenger compartment and engine; this, in turn, would be suspended within a vast, inverted wing form, to assist airflow both above and beneath the car. This 'floating' central cell is seamlessly divided into two halves: a transparent upper section and a lower section which acts as a structural aerodynamic skirt. The large transparent area serves two purposes, as it not only allows outstanding visibility for the car's occupants, but also showcases many of the MC12's exotic mechanicals including its pushrod-operated suspension and the V12's beautifully crafted carbon-fiber inlet trumpets.

Now you're probably also wondering why this

This is not a model. It actually drives. The front body section opens up like a clam shell to admit the driver

" The car made its driving debut at "
the Goodwood Festival of Speed
in the UK [pictured above]

car is called a Birdcage. No, it's not because it uses sandpaper for carpets (it doesn't), but because in the late 1950s and early '60s Maserati built a series of successful, Pininfarina-designed customer sports racers which were dubbed 'Birdcage' because they had complex spaceframe chassis made from about 200 radically triangulated, small diameter aluminum tubes. The cars were heinously time-consuming and expensive to manufacture, but in a pre-carbon-fiber world Maserati considered this to be the pinnacle of lightweight, high-strength chassis technology.

Not being cars to let their talents go unnoticed, the front-engined 250bhp, 170mph Tipo 61 and mid-engined Tipo 63 left parts of their chassis and other mechanicals in full view under an unusually large, transparent front windshield, much like the 2005 Birdcage 75th does today.

The front of the Birdcage 75th features the world's first homologated LED headlamps, with the lamp housings milled from solid blocks of aluminum that double as cooling ducts for the heat-intensive LEDs. The aluminum alloy wheels (20" front and 22" rear) are so intricate that they virtually defy description, so suffice to say they were specifically designed to evoke Maserati's Trident logo, and are secured with a single center-locking wheel nut.

The rear features a deep aerodynamic diffuser and active panels that move up and down for the required downforce at any given speed. When raised, these panels reveal engine-bay cooling outlets, which also serve to lower the air pressure underneath the wing surface, and thus help create more downforce. The ultra-thin tail lights also utilize the latest LED technology, and feature additional, very narrow air outlets from the engine compartment. Between these, a pair of vertically-stacked, chrome-tipped exhaust tailpipes release more hot gas and a heart-stirring sound.

Inside, there's Alcantara trim, the now-traditional Maserati clock, a suspended head-up display, state-of-the-art online Motorola communications systems and a centrally-mounted device for navigating through an assortment of menus and functions. On-board cameras can record the driving experience while infrared projectors give a transparent head-up display for enhanced night driving. ▨

The Maserati Birdcage 75th was first shown at the 2005 Geneva Motor Show, where it received the Best Concept award, and then made its driving debut at the Goodwood Festival of Speed in the UK four months later. It may have a peculiar name, but once seen, it will surely never be forgotten. ▨

SPECIFICATION	
ENGINE TYPE	V12
DISPLACEMENT	5,998cc (366 cu in)
POWER	700+bhp
TORQUE	490lb/ft (estimated)
TRANSMISSION	Six-speed 'Cambiocorsa' sequential manual
0-62mph	3.5 seconds (estimated)
TOP SPEED	205mph-plus (estimated)
PRICE	Money can't buy it
www.maserati.com	

The large transparent top section gives great visibility and shows off some of the car's exotic mechanical components

> " The elegance of a high-end limousine " combined with the power of a supercar

Maybach
Exelero

Last but definitely not least in this assembly of ultimate automobiles, if you think the Exelero looks like a million dollars, that's no surprise. In fact, it cost an awful lot more

The imposing Maybach Exelero has all the presence, power, grandeur and exclusivity befitting our final entry, and even if by now you're slightly jaded by the preceding collection of incredible cars, the Exelero won't fail to impress.

Combining the elegance and quality of a high-end limousine with the power and dynamism of a GT supercar, the Exelero was never intended for production. It was created to showcase the new ultra-high performance Exelero tire range from German manufacturer Fulda, a GoodYear/Dunlop affiliate.

Maybach and Fulda decided to go ahead and build the Exelero in 2003 and, as its basis, the car uses the chassis, engine and mechanicals of a Maybach 57 limo. The Exelero's body was designed by staff and students from Pforzheim Polytechnic's Department of Transport Design working with DaimlerChrysler's Sindelfingen design center.

To give the car a genuine coupe appearance, the Maybach limo's driving position had to be shifted rearwards by 40 centimeters (15.7 inches). In order to do this, the steering column, pedals and gear shift had to be relocated, which in turn meant installing a second front bulkhead.

The stock V12 bi-turbo motor also benefited from a little fettling; displacement is up from 5,513cc (336 cu in) to 5,908cc (360 cu in) and this combines with bigger turbochargers and intercooler, plus a larger radiator. Consequently, horsepower is raised

from 550 to 691bhp, with torque rising from 663 to 752lb/ft. Following innumerable wind-tunnel tests on models, the Exelero was built by the specialist vehicle manufacturer Stola of Turin, Italy.

Although the Exelero has no shortage of power, for a car some 16 centimeters (6.3 inches) wider than the standard 57 limo and measuring 5.9 meters (19.3 feet) in length, and weighing 2,660 kg (5,864lb) bone dry, you might not expect its performance to be particularly impressive. Wrong!

In May, 2005 at Italy's 7.77-mile Nardo test track, the Exelero recorded 215mph on its first lap and 218.38mph on its second. Granted, for this high-speed work the Exelero had its air-conditioning deactivated, its panel gaps taped over, its wheel spokes covered with low-drag discs and its 315/25 ZR23 tire pressures pumped up to just over 52psi. It also averaged 2.4mpg and burnt up over 3.2 gallons of 110-octane racing fuel per lap. However, nearly 220mph speeds from a near 3-ton luxury car is impressive by any standards.

The Exelero's 11 x 23-inch show-only wheels (as

From whichever angle you view it, the Maybach Exelero exudes menace, power and intent. The bi-turbo V12 can push this three-ton luxury automobile to nearly 220mph

seen here) are worth a mention, too. Weighing 23kg (50.7lb) apiece, they were each milled from a solid alloy block that started off weighing 257kg (566.6lb). So, for a set of four, there would have been 936kg (2,063.5lb) of aluminum swarf left to sweep from the machine shop floor! Inside each rear wheel is a 355mm (14-inch) rotor with one 4-piston caliper, while up front there are internally ventilated 376mm (14.8-inch) discs, each with two 4-piston calipers.

Interestingly, the Exelero does not represent the first time that Maybach and Fulda have teamed up to build a car. Back in 1938 the companies combined to create another high performance vehicle designed to demonstrate tire technology, and this was based on a Maybach SW 38.

Then, as now, one of the biggest challenges for tire makers is ever-increasing speeds, a situation polarized in the Germany of the late-'30s by the country's new, high speed autobahn network. Fulda needed a vehicle that could regularly test at over 125mph and so contracted Dörr and Schreck, a specialist car maker in Frankfurt, who in turn teamed up with Maybach and renowned aerodynamic specialist Freiherr Reinhard Koenig Fachsenfeld.

The result was the W38 Stromlinienfahrzeug (streamliner) of 1939. With a 140bhp, 3.8-liter (231 cubic inch) straight-six engine and a pre-selector 4-speed manual transmission, it easily fulfilled Fulda's brief. Its aerodynamic drag co-efficient was also impressive, at just 0.25 (0.6 was usual for series-production cars in those days, and even the Exelero has a poorer rating, at 0.28).

By comparison, a production SW 38, a powerful car in its day, was much slower, with a 99mph top speed with a 0-60mph time of around 27 seconds. However, with World War II looming, the W38 streamliner saw limited use and in the ensuing chaos the test vehicle disappeared. Its whereabouts remain a mystery to this day.

If that streamliner was unearthed today, it would certainly have considerable value on the collectors market, though probably nothing like the five million euros (£3.4m or $5.9m approx) that the Exelero is rumored to have cost. Still, for a car with its macho credentials and Darth Vader looks, the Exelero's worth is surely priceless. ✕

SPECIFICATION	
ENGINE TYPE	V12 turbocharged
DISPLACEMENT	5,908cc (360 cu in)
POWER	691bhp @ 5,000rpm
TORQUE	752lb/ft @ 2,500rpm
TRANSMISSION	Five-speed auto
0-62mph	4.4 seconds
TOP SPEED	218mph
PRICE	Not made to be sold
www.maybach-manufaktur.com	

The Exelero's styling echoes that of a car from Maybach's history, the 1939 W38 streamliner (above, left)

Road Car Records

Cars can be 'ultimates' for a number of reasons,
but some have numbers to back them up. Here are
a few (all street legal) with the figures to prove it.

HIGHEST TOP SPEED	248.5mph; Bugatti Veyron; 7,993cc (488 cu in) turbocharged W16, 987bhp
FASTEST SEDAN	217.6mph; Brabus E-Class; V12 Biturbo 6,700cc (408 cu in) turbocharged V12, 640bhp
FASTEST 'SOFT-TOP'	221.84mph; Sportec 911 Turbo Cabriolet SP580; 3,600cc (220 cu in) turbocharged 6cyl, 580bhp
FASTEST SUV	191.66mph; Sportec Cayenne Turbo SP600M; 4,511cc (275 cu in) turbocharged V8, 600bhp
QUICKEST 0-62MPH	2.46 seconds; Bugatti Veyron; 7,993cc (488 cu in) turbocharged W16, 987bhp
QUICKEST 0-100-0MPH	9.8 seconds; Ultima GTR640; 6,180cc (377cu in) V8, 641bhp
HIGHEST LATERAL G-FORCE	1.4g; Pagani Zonda F; 7,291cc (445 cu in) V12, 602bhp
HIGHEST POWER OUTPUT	1,046bhp; SSC Ultimate Aero; 387.2 cu in (6,348cc) supercharged V8
HIGHEST POWER-TO-WEIGHT RATIO	873.9 bhp per tonne; SSC Ultimate Aero; 387.2 cu in (6,348cc) supercharged V8, 1,046bhp
MOST EXPENSIVE	Bugatti Veyron; Retail Price: €1,160,000 (approx. £800,000/$1,412,000) + local taxes
FASTEST LAP OF NÜRBURGRING'S NORDSCHLEIFE CIRCUIT	6 minutes 56 seconds; Radical SR8: 2,600cc (159 cu in) V8, 363bhp

All figures correct at the time of going to press.
While every effort has been made to ensure accuracy, objects in your mirror may be closer than they seem.